Cape May Cooks

Cape May Cooks

Recipes from New Jersey's
Restaurant Capital

Connie Correia Fisher and Joanne Correia

small potatoes press

For Holden

To the world you might be just one person,
but to one person you might just be the world.

I'll always remember your first day on the beach.
June 26, 2002, Cape May, NJ

ISBN: 0-9661200-4-3
Library of Congress Control Number: 2002093378

Printed in the United States

Small Potatoes Press
1106 Stokes Avenue
Collingswood, NJ 08108
856-869-5207
www.smallpotatoespress.com

Although the author, editor, and publisher have made every effort to ensure the accuracy and completeness of information contained in this book, we assume no responsibility for errors, inaccuracies, omissions, or any inconsistency herein.

ATTENTION ORGANIZATIONS, SCHOOLS, AND EDUCATIONAL FACILITIES:

Quantity discounts are available on bulk purchases of this book for educational purposes or fund-raising. Special books or book excerpts can also be created to fit specific needs.

Foreword

Cape May is known for its bountiful restaurants, and you will find them here, the grandeur of The Washington Inn, the eclectic dining at Waters Edge, the sheer creativity of Daniel's on Broadway. But just as impressive are the historic town's inns and bed and breakfasts, providing customers with comfort, history, and lodging along quiet tree-lined streets and broad avenues with ocean views.

Fantasies of architecture and art comprise Cape May's inns, from the grand feel of The Mainstay to the history, breakfasts, and comfort of The Chalfonte Hotel, Inn at 22 Jackson, Queen Victoria, Southern Mansion, and numerous others.

Connie Fisher, known for her eclectic and thorough collections on food and dining in the Delaware Valley, takes us on a unique tour of Cape May's inns and restaurants. Make your reservations now.

Ed Hitzel
Publisher of Ed Hitzel's Restaurant Magazine,
Newsletter and Radio Show

Contents

Introduction . . . 7

Brunch . . . 8

Tea Time . . . 50

Social Hour . . . 76

Starters, Soups & Salads . . . 88

Entrees . . . 104

Side Dishes & Sauces . . . 124

Desserts . . . 134

Index . . . 151

"A body on vacation tends to remain on vacation
unless acted upon by an outside force."

Carol Reichel

Introduction

Cape May, a charming town filled with gaslights, gingerbread, and gables, has been welcoming visitors for more than a century. I fell in love it with some 30 years ago.

I loved it as a child when my family made yearly visits to Aunt Vi's house in search of horseshoe crabs and the prized Cape May diamonds. I loved it in my twenties when my husband and I would escape to Cape May for great food and romantic bed and breakfast weekends. I love it now, in my thirties, as I watch my baby boy crawl across the smooth Cape May sand and take his first, not-so-tentative, dip in the ocean.

Cape May actually inspired my first career goal. After a trip to town when I was 13, I announced that I wanted to own a bed and breakfast. I subscribed to *Country Inn* magazine and even got a degree in Hotel and Restaurant Management. But a few decidedly unglamorous industry jobs made me realize that it might be more fun to *stay* at a beautiful bed and breakfast or *eat* at a gourmet restaurant than to own one. Turns out, it is certainly more fun (for me, that is) to write about them.

Since the 1980s, writers have flocked to Cape May and praised the Cape May food scene. The *New York Times* even called Cape May "the restaurant capital of New Jersey." You'll agree when you sample the fabulous recipes I've collected from Cape May's best chefs and innkeepers. But there's more to Cape May than top-notch cuisine. There are people behind those restaurants, inns, hotels, and — let's not forget — the candy stores. The fishermen, laundry ladies, prep cooks, and waiters who are working hard while I'm lazing on the beach or riding my bike through the fall leaves. People who decorate the town to the hilt at Christmas and garden with gusto in the spring. These are the people who live and work in Cape May and have built the town's reputation with their toil and talent.

So thank you, Cape May, for the memories, the inspiration, the possibilities.

Bon appetit,
Connie Correia Fisher
Cherry Hill, NJ (Just two hours from Cape May!)

Brunch

Poached Eggs on Brioche with Caramelized Onions
Eggs Mey
Eggs Florentine
Egg Baskets
Sunrise Casserole
Swiss Custard
Baked Swiss Cheese Omelet
Ham and Broccoli Frittata
Smoked Turkey and Cheese Quiche
Four Cheese Herb Quiche
Caramelized Onion, Spinach, and Bacon Quiche
Fresh Corn Quiche
Ham and Cheese Croissants
Peach French Toast
Banana Bread French Toast
Orange Toast
French Toast Strata
Oven Baked Apple French Toast
Honey Baked French Toast
Walnut-encrusted French Toast
Peach Pillows
Ginger Pancakes with Lemon Sauce
Ricotta Pancakes
Whole Wheat Apple Pancakes
German Apple Pancakes
Fruit Pizza
Fruits of Summer Souffle
Citrus Sections in Vanilla Marinade
Poached Peaches with White Cheese Mousse
Baked Peaches with Crunch Topping
Granola Delight
Banana Chocolate Chip Muffins
Monstrous Sour Cream Muffins
Orange Walnut Muffins
Bannoch Bread
Habit Forming Cinnamon Buns
Strawberry Butter
Blueberry Compote

Poached Eggs on Brioche with Caramelized Onions

Barbara Bray Wilde, Innkeeper
The Southern Mansion Bed & Breakfast

4 tablespoons butter
½ medium onion, sliced
1 teaspoon minced garlic
2 tablespoons sugar
2 tablespoons white wine
1 sprig thyme
Black pepper to taste
4 large eggs
1 tablespoon vinegar
Butter, softened
4 slices brioche

Melt butter in a sauté pan. Add onion, garlic, sugar, white wine, thyme, and pepper and sauté until onions are brown but not burned.

Meanwhile, bring 2 to 3 inches of water to boiling in a saucepan or a deep omelet pan. Reduce heat to keep water gently simmering. Break cold eggs, one at a time, into a custard cup or break several into a bowl. Holding dish close to water's surface, slip eggs, one by one, into water. Cook until whites are completely set and yolks begin to thicken but are not hard, about 3 to 5 minutes. With a slotted spoon, lift out eggs. Drain in spoon or on paper towels.

Butter, then grill brioche in a sauté pan or on a grill. Place one egg on each slice of brioche and cover with caramelized onions.

SERVES 4

Eggs Mey

George and Kathleen Blinn, Innkeepers
Captain Mey's Bed & Breakfast Inn

4 ounces cream cheese

2 ounces Neufchatel (lower fat) cream cheese

10 eggs

5 ounces evaporated milk

1 tablespoon chopped fresh dill

Salt to taste

2 tablespoons butter

1 tablespoon vegetable oil

Dice cream cheeses into ¼-inch cubes. Combine with eggs, evaporated milk, dill, and salt in a mixing bowl.

Melt butter in a large frying pan over medium heat. Add oil. Pour in egg mixture. Fold mixture — do not stir — until mixture is set and cooked through. Serve hot.

SERVES 4 TO 6

Captain Mey's Bed & Breakfast Inn

Web site: www.captainmeys.com

Open: all year

Serves: breakfast and afternoon tea

Known for: named after Captain Cornelius Mey, the Dutch sailor who explored this area in 1621

Most requested room: rooms with romantic whirlpool tubs for two

Years in Business: 22

Eggs Florentine

Sandra J. Miller, Owner/Innkeeper
Windward House Inn Bed and Breakfast

3 tablespoons butter
3 tablespoons flour
1 tablespoon salt
½ teaspoon oregano
⅛ teaspoon pepper
1½ cups milk
12 tablespoons water
12 eggs
10 ounces frozen chopped spinach
¼ cup grated Parmesan cheese

Preheat oven to 350°. Spray a 12-cup muffin pan and a 9 x 13-inch baking dish with nonstick spray.

Melt butter in a skillet over medium heat. Add flour, salt, oregano, and pepper. Mix well with a wire whisk. Let simmer until bubbling, lowering heat, if necessary. Add milk and cook, stirring frequently, until thickened. (Add more milk if you prefer a thinner sauce.) Lower heat to keep warm and reserve.

Place 1 tablespoon water in each cup in muffin pan. Break 1 egg into each cup. Bake for 15 to 20 minutes.

Meanwhile, steam spinach according to package directions. Drain well and keep warm.

Arrange spinach evenly in bottom of baking dish. Top with oven-poached eggs. Top eggs with white sauce and sprinkle with Parmesan cheese. Put on center rack in oven and broil until cheese is a light brown.

SERVES 8

Egg Baskets

Joe and JoAnne Tornambe, Innkeepers
Woodleigh House B&B

8 slices bread
Butter
8 thin slices ham
8 ounces shredded Cheddar cheese
8 eggs

Preheat oven to 325°.

Remove crusts from bread. Roll slices flat with a rolling pin. Butter one side of each slice. Press slices, buttered side down, into muffin tins. Bake for 10 minutes. (Bread baskets can be stored in freezer and saved for future use.)

Cut ham into rounds and fit into bread baskets. Sprinkle with half of cheese. Carefully crack an egg into each basket. Top with remaining cheese. Dot with butter. Bake for 15 minutes. Enjoy!

SERVES 8

Woodleigh House B&B

Web site: www.woodleighhouse.com

Open: all year

Known for: beautiful gardens, warm and friendly atmosphere, and delicious breakfasts

Most requested room: William and Mary Suite

Years in Business: 5

Sunrise Casserole

Cynthia and Tom Riker, Innkeepers
The Puffin

1 pound lean bulk sausage
2 large red apples, cored, peeled, and thinly sliced
5 eggs, beaten
1½ cups milk
6 to 7 bread slices, crusts removed and bread cubed
1 cup grated sharp Cheddar cheese
½ teaspoon dry mustard

Brown sausage in a skillet. Reserve fat. Put sausage in a 13 x 9 x 2-inch glass baking dish. Sauté apples in reserved fat. Spread over sausage.

Combine remaining ingredients in a mixing bowl. Pour over sausage and apples. Cover with foil and refrigerate over night.

When ready to serve, preheat oven to 350°. Bake covered for 30 minutes. Remove foil and continue baking for 20 minutes. Let stand for 5 to 10 minutes before serving.

SERVES 8

The Puffin

Web site: www.beachcomber.com/Capemay/Guest/puffin.html

Open: seasonally

Known for: great wraparound porch, comfortable casualness

Most requested room: Atlantic Suite

Years in Business: 6½

Swiss Custard

Cynthia and Tom Riker, Innkeepers
The Puffin

6 slices firm white bread
Butter, softened
5 eggs
2 cups light cream
⅛ teaspoon salt
⅛ teaspoon dry mustard
2 cups shredded Swiss cheese
Fresh parsley, chopped
Fresh chives, chopped
Fresh garlic, minced

Spread bread with butter. Push each slice into a ramekin or custard cup.

Beat eggs until light. Mix in cream, salt, and mustard. Sprinkle cheese over bread. Pour egg mixture over cheese. Sprinkle with herbs and garlic.

Cover and chill at least 30 minutes or overnight.

When ready to serve, preheat oven to 350°. Bake uncovered for 30 minutes or until set and puffed up. Serve at once.

SERVES 6

Baked Swiss Cheese Omelet

Don Schweikert, Innkeeper
Saltwood House Bed & Breakfast

10 ounces Swiss cheese, grated (approximately 2½ cups)
2 tablespoons butter
1 cup heavy cream
12 eggs, lightly beaten
Dash of pepper

Preheat oven to 340°. Grease a 13 x 9 x 2-inch baking dish.

Spread cheese over bottom of baking dish. Dot with butter. Pour half of heavy cream over cheese. Top with eggs and then remaining heavy cream. Sprinkle with pepper. Bake for 40 to 50 minutes or until set.

SERVES 8

Saltwood House Bed & Breakfast

Web site: www.saltwoodhouse.com

Open: seasonally

Serves: brunch and afternoon tea

Known for: peach color

Most requested room: Saratoga Room

Years in Business: 8

Ham and Broccoli Frittata

Lynda and Corbin Cogswell, Innkeepers
The Linda Lee Bed and Breakfast

2 tablespoons butter
2 cups diced cooked ham (about 8 ounces)
1 medium onion, diced
2½ cups chopped fresh broccoli
1 teaspoon salt
¾ teaspoon pepper
12 large eggs
½ cup sour cream
¼ teaspoon baking powder
6 plum tomatoes, seeded and chopped
2 cups grated sharp Cheddar cheese (about 8 ounces)
½ cup chopped fresh basil

Preheat oven to 350°.

Melt butter in a 12-inch ovenproof skillet. Add ham, onion, and broccoli and sauté for 5 minutes over medium heat. Stir in salt and pepper.

Beat together eggs, sour cream, and baking powder, using an electric mixer at medium speed, for 2 or 3 minutes. Pour over ham mixture.

Bake for 15 minutes. Remove from oven and sprinkle with tomato, cheese, and basil. Bake for 15 to 20 minutes or until set. Serve immediately.

SERVES 8

The Linda Lee Bed and Breakfast

Web site: www.thelindalee.com

Open: all year

Serves: brunch and afternoon tea

Known for: friendly, homey atmosphere

Most requested room: Uncle Teddy's Garden Room

Years in Business: 5

Smoked Turkey and Cheese Quiche

Kathy Mendolia and Sue Kulman, Innkeepers
Velia's Seaside Inn

1 cup cubed smoked turkey breast
1 cup frozen broccoli florets, thawed and drained thoroughly
1 cup grated white Cheddar cheese
1 unbaked pie shell
4 eggs
1 cup milk
1 teaspoon dry mustard
½ teaspoon salt
½ teaspoon pepper

Preheat oven to 375°.
Layer turkey, broccoli, and cheese in pie shell.
    Combine remaining ingredients in a bowl and beat well. Pour over layered ingredients. Bake for 35 to 45 minutes. Let stand for 10 minutes before serving.

SERVES 6

Velia's Seaside Inn

Innkeepers: Kathy Mendolia and Sue Kulman
Favorite Foods: seafood
Favorite Cape May Activity: walking on the beach

Four Cheese Herb Quiche

Lynda and Corbin Cogswell, Innkeepers
The Linda Lee Bed and Breakfast

½ cup shredded Swiss cheese
½ cup shredded Cheddar cheese
½ cup shredded mozzarella cheese
1 9 or 10-inch prepared pie shell
5 eggs
1 cup light cream
½ cup ricotta cheese
1 teaspoon each dried dill, parsley, and ground onion
1 teaspoon fresh or dried chives
½ teaspoon dried thyme

Preheat oven to 400°.

Combine Swiss, Cheddar, and mozzarella cheeses and place in pie shell. Blend remaining ingredients in a blender on high for 2 minutes. Pour over cheeses. Bake for 60 minutes or until top is lightly brown and firm.

SERVES 6

Caramelized Onion, Spinach and Bacon Quiche

Sally Denithorne, Innkeeper
The Primrose Inn

3 cups sliced white onions
1 (10 ounces) can refrigerated pizza crust
1 (10 ounces) package frozen chopped spinach, thawed, drained, and
  squeezed dry
¼ cup low-fat sour cream
2 tablespoons minced shallots
1 cup evaporated skim milk
¼ teaspoon salt
⅛ teaspoon pepper
2 large egg whites
1 large egg
⅓ cup chopped Canadian bacon
¼ cup shredded reduced-fat Monterey Jack cheese

Heat onions in a sauté pan over medium-high heat and cook, stirring
frequently, until brown (not burned) and caramelized.

Preheat oven to 350°. Spray a 9-inch pie plate with nonstick spray.

Remove dough from package and shape into a 4-inch circle. Cover and
let stand for 5 minutes. Roll dough into an 11-inch circle on a lightly
floured surface. Fit dough into prepared pie plate and flute edges.

The Primrose Inn

Web site: www.theprimroseinn.com

Open: all year

Serves: brunch and afternoon tea

Known for: great breakfasts and hospitality

Most requested room: Nana Lambert's Room and Sarah's Suite

Years in Business: 5

Combine spinach, sour cream, and shallots in a small bowl. In a separate bowl, combine evaporated milk, salt, pepper, egg whites, and egg and stir well with a whisk. Stir ⅓ cup milk mixture into spinach mixture. Spoon spinach mixture into bottom of prepared crust. Add caramelized onions and top with bacon and cheese. Pour remaining milk mixture over cheese. Place pie plate on a baking sheet and bake for 45 minutes or until set. Let stand 10 minutes before serving.

SERVES 6

Fresh Corn Quiche

**Tom and Sue Carroll, Innkeepers
The Mainstay Inn**

3 eggs
1 (¼-inch) slice onion
1 tablespoon sugar
1 tablespoon all-purpose flour
1 teaspoon salt
3 tablespoons butter, melted
1⅓ cups half-and-half, scalded
2 cups uncooked fresh corn or frozen, thawed
1 (9-inch) piecrust, unbaked

Preheat oven to 375°.

In a food processor, combine eggs, onion, sugar, flour, and salt. Add butter and half-and-half and blend. Fold in corn.

Pour mixture into piecrust and bake for 45 minutes or until slightly puffed up and lightly browned. Cut into wedges and serve immediately.

SERVES 6 TO 8

The Mainstay Inn

Innkeepers: Tom and Sue Carroll
Favorite Foods: seafood
Favorite Cape May Activity: eating in restaurants

Ham and Cheese Croissants

Cindy Franklin, Innkeeper
Inn by the Silver Maple

4 croissants
4 eggs
1 cup milk
1 teaspoon Worcestershire sauce
16 thinly sliced pieces lunchmeat ham
1½ cups shredded Cheddar cheese
Chopped fresh parsley

Preheat over to 350°. Grease a shallow baking dish.

Slice croissants in half lengthwise. Beat eggs, milk, and Worcestershire until blended and smooth. Pour egg mixture into a separate baking dish and lay croissants in mixture, sliced sides down. Soak for 1 hour.

Place 4 croissants halves in prepared baking dish. Cover each half with 4 slices ham, ¼ cup cheese, and remaining croissant half. Bake for 30 minutes. In final 5 minutes, top with remaining cheese and parsley.

(Fruit or veggies may be substituted for ham to make great veggie croissants.)

SERVES 4

Inn by the Silver Maple

Web site: www.capemay.com/silvermaple.com

Open: all year

Serves: breakfast

Known for: hearty breakfast, cleanliness, elegant but casual atmosphere

Most requested room: Sawyer

Years in Business: 5

Peach French Toast

Carrie O'Sullivan, Innkeeper
Victorian Lace Inn

1½ cups light brown sugar, packed
½ cup butter
1 (29 ounces) can sliced peaches
10 thick slices French bread
5 eggs
½ cup milk
1 tablespoon vanilla
Cinnamon
Confectioners' sugar

Grease an 8½ x 13-inch microwave-safe pan.

Place brown sugar and butter in pan. Microwave for 1 minute or until butter melts. Mix butter and brown sugar thoroughly.

Drain peaches. Place peach slices over brown sugar mixture. Top peaches with bread slices.

In a separate bowl, combine eggs, milk, and vanilla. Beat on low for 1 minute or until well combined. Pour evenly over bread. Sprinkle with cinnamon to taste. Cover and refrigerate overnight.

Preheat oven to 350°. Bake uncovered for 45 minutes. Sprinkle with confectioners' sugar and serve.

SERVES 10

Banana Bread French Toast

Elizabeth and Niels Favre, Innkeepers
Canterbury Cottage Inn B&B

1 loaf Banana Bread (Recipe appears on page 75.)
4 large eggs
¼ cup whipping or heavy cream
2 tablespoons brown sugar, packed
1 teaspoon vanilla extract
¼ teaspoon ground cinnamon
¼ teaspoon ground nutmeg
3 tablespoons butter
Maple syrup

Preheat oven on lowest setting possible.

Cut bread into 12 slices. In a large bowl, whisk remaining ingredients, except butter and syrup, until well blended.

Melt 1 tablespoon butter in a large heavy skillet over medium heat. Place some bread in batter and turn to coat thoroughly. Place bread in skillet and cook until golden brown, about 3 minutes on each side.

Transfer cooked slices to a cookie sheet and keep warm in oven. Repeat process until all slices are cooked. Serve with maple syrup.

SERVES 6

Canterbury Cottage Inn B&B

Web site: www.canterburycottageinn.com

Open: all year

Serves: brunch and afternoon tea

Known for: our five-course served breakfast

Most requested room: Pembroke

Years in Business: 5

Orange Toast

Betty and Frank Boclair, Innkeepers
Beauclaire's Bed & Breakfast

8 slices dense bread, each ¾-inch thick
4 whole eggs
7 ounces whole milk
¼ cup Triple Sec liqueur
½ teaspoon vanilla extract
½ teaspoon orange extract
2 tablespoons sugar
½ teaspoon baking powder
½ teaspoon cinnamon
½ teaspoon nutmeg
Confectioners' sugar
Orange slices

Place bread slices in a 9 x 13-inch pan.

Beat eggs until light. Add milk, Triple Sec, and extracts. In a separate bowl, combine all dry ingredients. Add wet ingredients to dry and mix well. Pour over bread. Turn bread over once to wet both sides. Cover and refrigerate overnight.

When ready to serve, fry each slice on a hot griddle for approximately 4 minutes per side or until golden. Sprinkle with confectioners' sugar and garnish with orange slices.

SERVES 4

Beauclaire's Bed & Breakfast

Web site: www.beauclaires.com

Open: all year

Known for: beautiful Queen Ann built in 1879

Most requested room: Room #1

Years in Business: 5

French Toast Strata

Ed and Diane Hutchinson, Owners/Innkeepers
Fairthorne Bed & Breakfast

1 loaf day-old Italian or French bread, cubed
8 ounces cream cheese
1 cup fresh or frozen blueberries (or raisins, if you prefer)
Cinnamon to taste
9 eggs
2 egg yolks
2½ cups half-and-half
¾ cup sugar
8 tablespoons butter, melted
Blueberry Compote (Recipe appears on page 49.)

Spray a 9 x 13-inch baking dish with nonstick spray.

Place cubed bread in prepared dish and arrange in an even layer. Dot with cream cheese and blueberries. Sprinkle with cinnamon.

Blend eggs, yolks, half-and-half, sugar, and butter in a large blender or mixing bowl. Pour over bread. Cover and refrigerate overnight.

When ready to serve, preheat oven to 350°. Bake for about 45 minutes. Let stand for 10 minutes before serving. Serve as is or with blueberry compote.

SERVES 8

Fairthorne Bed & Breakfast

Web site: www.fairthorne.com

Open: all year

Serves: breakfast and afternoon tea

Known for: warm hospitality

Most requested room: Edwina and Ashley

Years in Business: 10

Oven Baked Apple French Toast

Jan and Mark Pask, Innkeepers
Luther Ogden Inn

1 cup brown sugar, packed
½ cup butter
¼ cup maple syrup
3 apples, peeled and sliced
1 loaf French bread
5 eggs
1½ cups milk
1 tablespoon vanilla extract
½ teaspoon nutmeg
1 teaspoon cinnamon
½ cup raisins

Cook sugar, butter, and syrup over medium-low heat for 5 minutes. Pour into a 9 x 13-inch baking dish. Arrange apple slices over syrup mixture.

Slice bread into ¾-inch-thick slices. Arrange over apples.

Whisk together eggs, milk, vanilla extract, nutmeg, and cinnamon. Pour over bread. Top with raisins. Cover and refrigerate overnight.

When ready to serve, preheat oven to 350°. Bake, uncovered, for 50 minutes. To serve, flip bread over so that apples are on top.

SERVES 8

Luther Ogden Inn

Web site: www.lutherogdeninn.com

Open: all year **Serves:** breakfast

Known for: homemade breakfast on the wraparound porch

Most requested room: Room 2

Years in Business: 5

Innkeepers' Favorite Foods: mint chocolate chip ice cream, shrimp, monkey bread

Honey Baked French Toast

Kate Emerson, Owner/Innkeeper
Abigail Adams Bed & Breakfast By The Sea

14 eggs
1½ pints heavy cream
½ cup honey
¼ teaspoon nutmeg
1 loaf French bread, cut into 10 slices
Confectioners' sugar
Maple sugar

Grease a 9 x 13-inch baking pan. Mix together first 4 ingredients. Dip bread slices into egg mixture and arrange in pan. Pour remaining egg mixture over bread, cover, and refrigerate overnight.

When ready to bake, preheat oven to 350°. Turn over bread slices to make sure egg mixture penetrated through bread. Bake for 1 hour. Dust with confectioners' sugar and serve with maple syrup.

SERVES 8

Abigail Adams Bed & Breakfast by the Sea

Web site: www.abigailadamsinn.com

Open: all year

Serves: breakfast and afternoon tea

Known for: located 100 feet from Cape May's prettiest beaches

Most requested room: "President John Adams" Room

Years in Business: 18

Walnut-encrusted French Toast

Barbara Bray Wilde, Innkeeper
The Southern Mansion Bed & Breakfast

8 eggs
½ cup heavy cream
4 teaspoons bourbon
2 teaspoons walnut extract
2 teaspoons vanilla extract
½ cup sugar
2 teaspoons cinnamon
½ cup finely chopped walnuts
8 thick slices bread
Butter
Maple syrup

Heat an electric griddle or skillet over medium heat.

Whisk eggs. Stir in cream, bourbon, extracts, sugar, and cinnamon. Add walnuts. (The mix should be thick.) Dip bread into egg mixture, making sure plenty of walnuts stick to the bread.

Lightly coat hot griddle with butter. Brown bread on both sides. Serve hot with maple syrup.

SERVES 4

The Southern Mansion Bed & Breakfast

Innkeeper: Barbara Bray Wilde

Favorite Foods: southeast Asian

Favorite Cape May Activity: going out to dinner

Peach Pillows

Cindy and James Schmucker, Innkeepers
Bedford Inn

4 small croissants
3 ounces cream cheese, softened
1 large peach, peeled and thinly sliced
1 cup milk or half-and-half
2 eggs
Dash of cinnamon
Dash of nutmeg

Split croissants in half lengthwise. Spread cream cheese on bottom halves. Place peach slices evenly on cream cheese. Cover with top halves. Whisk together remaining ingredients.

Heat griddle or large skillet over medium heat. Dip each croissant in egg mixture. Cook croissants on each side until golden brown. (Cook slowly so the middle gets hot.) Serve immediately or keep covered in a 300° oven until ready to serve.

SERVES 4

Bedford Inn
Innkeepers: Cindy and James Schmucker
Favorite Foods: pasta and seafood
Favorite Cape May Activity: relaxing!

Ginger Pancakes with Lemon Sauce

**Nancy and Dave McGonigle, Innkeepers
The Wooden Rabbit**

2 cups pancake mix
1 teaspoon cinnamon
1 teaspoon ground cloves
½ teaspoon ginger
1 egg
1½ cups milk
½ cup cream cheese, softened
Lemon Sauce (see recipe)

Combine all ingredients, except cream cheese and lemon sauce, and mix until smooth. Transfer mixture to a pitcher for easy pouring.

Grease heated griddle. Pour about 3 tablespoons batter per pancake onto hot griddle. Cook pancakes until puffed and dry around edges. Turn and cook until other side is golden brown.

Remove from griddle. Spread each pancake with a thin layer of cream cheese. Roll into a tube. Serve with lemon sauce.

SERVES 6

The Wooden Rabbit

Web site: www.woodenrabbit.com

Open: all year

Serves: breakfast and afternoon tea

Known for: oldest house on street, only Federal style B&B in Cape May

Most requested room: Plantation Suite and Albert Henry Hughes Suite

Years in Business: 4

Lemon Sauce

1 cup butter
2 eggs, beaten
2 cups sugar
½ cup water
6 tablespoons fresh lemon juice
Peel of 1 lemon, grated

Combine all ingredients in a heavy saucepan. Cook over medium heat, whisking often, until thickened. Remove from heat and keep warm until ready to serve.

Ricotta Pancakes

Cindy and James Schmucker, Innkeepers
Bedford Inn

4 large eggs, separated
2 cups ricotta cheese
⅔ cup sour cream
1⅓ cups flour
1 tablespoon baking powder
½ teaspoon salt
½ teaspoon baking soda
1½ cups whole milk
Melted butter
Maple syrup

Whisk together egg yolks, ricotta cheese, and sour cream in a large bowl to blend. In a separate bowl, whisk together flour, baking powder, salt, and baking soda. Add dry mixture to wet mixture and stir until combined. Stir in milk.

In a separate bowl, beat egg whites, using an electric mixer on medium speed, until soft peaks form. Fold beaten whites into batter.

Heat griddle or large skillet over medium heat. Brush heated griddle with butter. For each pancake, spoon 2 tablespoons batter onto griddle. Cook until golden brown, about 3 minutes per side. Serve with maple syrup.

YIELDS ABOUT 40 SMALL PANCAKES

Bedford Inn

Web site: www.bedfordinn.com

Open: April through December

Serves: brunch and afternoon tea

Known for: side-by-side mother-daughter Italianate Victorian

Most requested room: Virginia's Suite

Years in Business: 37

Whole Wheat Apple Pancakes

George and Kathleen Blinn, Innkeepers
Captain Mey's Bed & Breakfast Inn

1½ cups unbleached flour
1½ cups whole wheat flour
⅓ cup toasted wheat germ
3 tablespoons sugar
3 teaspoons baking powder
1½ teaspoons baking soda
¾ teaspoon salt
½ teaspoon cinnamon
¼ teaspoon nutmeg
3 eggs
3 cups buttermilk
¾ cup milk
1 teaspoon vanilla extract
6 tablespoons butter, melted and cooled

Combine all dry ingredients in a large bowl. In a separate bowl, lightly beat eggs, buttermilk, milk, vanilla, and melted butter. Add wet ingredients to dry ingredients all at once. Stir just enough to blend. (Do not over stir. Batter should be lumpy.)

Heat an electric griddle to 375° or a heavy skillet over medium-high heat. Lightly oil. Pour ¼-cupfuls batter onto griddle or skillet. Flip when bubbles appear on tops of pancakes and bottoms are lightly browned.

SERVES 8

German Apple Pancakes

Kate Emerson, Owner/Innkeeper
Abigail Adams Bed & Breakfast By The Sea

10 eggs
1 cup flour
1 teaspoon baking powder
⅛ teaspoon salt
2 cups milk
¼ cup butter, melted
2 teaspoons vanilla
2 tablespoons plus 1½ cups sugar
¼ teaspoon plus 1 teaspoon cinnamon
¼ teaspoon plus ¼ teaspoon nutmeg
½ cup butter
2 to 3 apples, peeled and thinly sliced

Blend together first 7 ingredients. Add 2 tablespoons sugar, ¼ teaspoon cinnamon, and ¼ teaspoon nutmeg. Reserve.

In a separate bowl, combine remaining sugar, cinnamon, and nutmeg. Reserve.

Preheat oven to 425°. Heat 2 large ovenproof skillets over medium heat on top of stove. Divide ½ cup butter between skillets and melt. Remove from heat.

Sprinkle half of sugar mixture over melted butter. Cover with apple slices and sprinkle with remaining sugar mixture. Return pans to heat and cook until bubbling, about 4 or 5 minutes. Pour batter over apples.

Transfer pans to oven and bake for 15 minutes. Reduce heat to 350° and continue baking for another 10 minutes or so.

SERVES 8

Fruit Pizza

Tom and Sue Carroll, Innkeepers
The Mainstay Inn

1 (14 ounces) can sweetened condensed milk

½ cup sour cream

¼ cup lemon juice

1 teaspoon vanilla

½ cup butter, softened

¼ cup brown sugar, packed

1 cup all-purpose flour

¼ cup quick-cooking rolled oats

¼ cup finely chopped walnuts

½ cup apricot preserves

2 tablespoons brandy

4 cups thinly sliced fresh fruit, such as kiwis, strawberries, and bananas

Mix milk, sour cream, lemon juice, and vanilla. Refrigerate for at least 30 minutes.

Preheat oven to 375°. Lightly oil a 12-inch pizza pan.

Beat butter and sugar until fluffy. Mix in flour, rolled oats, and walnuts. Place dough on prepared pizza pan and press into a circle, forming a rim around the edge. Prick with a fork and bake for 10 to 12 minutes. Cool.

Melt apricot preserves in a small saucepan over low heat. Add brandy and mix. Strain.

Spoon chilled mixture over prepared crust. Arrange fruit slices in a circular pattern over filling. Brush apricot glaze over fruit. Cover and refrigerate for 60 minutes. Cut into wedges and serve cold.

SERVES 8

Fruits of Summer Souffle

Ed and Diane Hutchinson, Owners/Innkeepers
Fairthorne Bed & Breakfast

⅓ cup plus 1½ tablespoons sugar
1 stick butter
4 extra large eggs plus 1 large egg
1½ cups sour cream
½ cup orange juice
1 cup flour
2 teaspoon baking powder
2 cups cottage cheese
8 ounces cream cheese, softened
1 teaspoon vanilla extract
Knott's Berry Farm Syrup
Fresh fruit (sliced strawberries, peaches, blueberries)

Preheat oven to 350°. Spray six 6-ounce ramekins with nonstick spray.

In a blender, mix ⅓ cup sugar, butter, 4 extra large eggs, sour cream, juice, flour, and baking powder. Reserve batter.

Blend remaining sugar, cottage cheese, cream cheese, 1 large egg, and vanilla with a mixer until filling is smooth.

Pour half of batter into ramekins. Spoon filling over batter and top with remaining batter. Bake for 40 to 45 minutes or until an inserted knife or toothpick comes out clean. Let cool for about 10 minutes. Drizzle with syrup and top with fresh fruit.

SERVES 6

Fairthorne Bed & Breakfast

Innkeepers: Ed and Diane Hutchinson
Favorite Foods: tuna steak at Daniels on Broadway
Favorite Cape May Activity: watching sunsets

Citrus Sections in Vanilla Marinade

Joe and Fran Geores, Innkeepers
The Inn at Journey's End

1⅓ cups water
⅔ cup sugar
1 tablespoon vanilla extract
4 large navel oranges
3 medium grapefruits

Combine water and sugar in a saucepan. Cook over medium heat, stirring until sugar dissolves. Add vanilla. Remove from heat and cool.

Clean and section oranges and grapefruits over a large bowl, catching juice. Add sections to juice in bowl. Pour cooled vanilla mixture over fruit. Cover and refrigerate overnight. Serve cold.

SERVES 8 TO 10

Poached Peaches with White Cheese Mousse

Sandra J. Miller, Owner/Innkeeper
Windward House Inn Bed and Breakfast

3 cups water
1½ cups sugar
⅓ cup lemon juice
1 tablespoon vanilla
6 medium peaches, halved and pitted
½ cup ricotta cheese
¼ cup low-fat cream cheese
3 tablespoons confectioners' sugar
1½ teaspoons lemon rind
½ teaspoon vanilla
Nutmeg

Combine first 4 ingredients in a large glass mixing bowl. Microwave on high for 10 minutes. Stir until sugar dissolves. Add peach halves to syrup and microwave on high for 4 minutes. Cover and refrigerate overnight.

Combine remaining ingredients, except nutmeg. Beat until well combined. Cover and refrigerate.

When ready to serve, place peach halves on serving plate, cut sides up. Spoon mousse into pit cavities and sprinkle with nutmeg.

SERVES 6

Windward House Inn

Web site: www.windwardhouseinn.com

Open: all year (almost)

Serves: brunch and afternoon tea

Known for: one of the most authentically decorated inns

Most requested room: Cottage Room

Years in Business: 25

Baked Peaches with Crunch Topping

Don Schweikert, Innkeeper
Saltwood House Bed & Breakfast

3 peaches, peeled, halved, and pitted
6 teaspoons plus ½ cup brown sugar, packed
4 tablespoons butter, softened
½ cup rolled oats
¼ cup flour

Preheat oven to 350°. Grease a 9 x 13–inch baking dish.

Place peach halves, cut sides up, in baking dish. Place 1 teaspoon brown sugar in each center.

Combine remaining ingredients. Fill centers with crunch topping. Bake for 10 minutes. Turn on broiler and broil for 2 minutes or just until crisp. Serve with vanilla yogurt or whipped cream.

SERVES 6

Saltwood House Bed & Breakfast

Innkeeper: Don Schweikert

Favorite Foods: pasta

Favorite Cape May Activity: going to the beach

Granola Delight

Deborah Longstreet, Innkeeper
The Sea Villa Hotel

3 to 4 small bananas
Juice of ½ lemon
1 cup banana or vanilla yogurt
1 cup ricotta cheese
1 egg
½ cup sugar
½ to 1 cup granola cereal mix
Strawberries, optional

Slice bananas and toss in lemon juice. Reserve.

Mix together yogurt, ricotta cheese, egg, and sugar. Pour half of granola into mixture.

Slowly fold in half of chopped bananas. Pour mixture into a trifle dish or dessert cups, alternating layers of yogurt mixture and remaining granola. Garnish with remaining bananas and, if desired, strawberries.

SERVES 6 TO 8

The Sea Villa Hotel

Open: seasonally

Serves: brunch and afternoon tea

Known for: fantastic location, charming and laid-back, dolphin watching

Most requested room: #1 with its beautiful 4 poster bed and great views of the beach

Years in Business: 8

Banana Chocolate Chip Muffins

Joe and Fran Geores, Innkeepers
The Inn at Journey's End

¾ cup brown sugar, packed
½ cup butter, softened
3 ripe medium-size bananas
2 eggs
1 teaspoon vanilla extract
1 cup all-purpose flour
1 cup whole wheat flour
1 teaspoon baking soda
¼ teaspoon salt
½ cup semi-sweet chocolate chips

Preheat oven to 350°. Grease twenty-four 2¾-inch muffin cups.

Cream together brown sugar and butter. Add bananas, eggs, and vanilla and beat until well mixed. Stir in flours, baking soda, and salt and mix until moistened. Fold in chocolate chips. Spoon into prepared muffin tins to about three-quarters full.

Bake for 15 minutes or until tester comes out clean.

YIELDS 24 MUFFINS

The Inn at Journey's End

Web site: www.innatjourneysend.com

Open: all year

Serves: breakfast and afternoon tea

Known for: our friendly and peaceful atmosphere, clawfoot tubs, and fabulous four-course breakfasts

Years in Business: 3½

Monstrous Sour Cream Muffins

David Biondi, Chef
Zoe's Restaurant

10 eggs
5 cups sour cream
5 cups whole milk
5 teaspoons vanilla
20 cups flour
5 cups sugar
½ cup plus 2 tablespoons baking powder
2½ teaspoons baking soda
2½ teaspoons salt
2½ cups butter, melted and cooled
5 to 6 cups fresh fruit of your choice, cleaned and cut into small chunks

Preheat oven to 325° to 350° Spray extra large muffin tins with nonstick spray. (Extra large tins are available at specialty stores. You will be making a total of 16 muffins.)

In a large mixing bowl, whisk together eggs, sour cream, milk, and vanilla. In a separate bowl, combine flour, sugar, baking powder, baking soda, and salt. Pour dry ingredients into wet and mix lightly. Add cooled melted butter and fruit.

Spoon batter into tins. Bake for 25 to 30 minutes or until tester comes out clean. (Muffins will puff up very large and taste wonderful.)

YIELDS 16 MUFFINS

Zoe's Restaurant

Chef: David Biondi

Chef's Training: five years on the jobs; currently a college senior

Hobbies: avid reader, plays guitar in a band

Favorite Foods: pasta, cheesesteaks, linguini and clams

Orange Walnut Muffins

Barbara Morris, Owner
The Henry Sawyer Inn

2¼ cups all-purpose flour

1½ cups sugar

1 (3.4 ounces) package instant vanilla pudding

3 teaspoons baking powder

1 teaspoon salt

¾ cup vegetable shortening

¾ cup plus 2½ tablespoons orange juice

4 eggs

1 teaspoon orange extract

½ teaspoon vanilla extract

1 cup chopped walnuts

½ cup confectioners' sugar

Grease 12 large-size muffin cups. Preheat oven to 350°.

Place all ingredients, except 2½ tablespoons orange juice and confectioners' sugar, in a large bowl. Mix with a hand mixer at medium speed until well blended, about 2 or 3 minutes. Spoon batter into prepared cups. Bake for 20 minutes or until an inserted cake tester comes out clean. Cool.

Combine remaining orange juice and confectioners' sugar and stir until smooth. Drizzle over each muffin.

YIELDS 12 MUFFINS

The Henry Sawyer Inn

Web site: www.henrysawyerinn.com

Open: all year

Serves: breakfast and afternoon tea

Known for: cradle made by Abraham Lincoln's father, Hummel collection, welcoming environment

Years in Business: 10

Bannoch Bread

Nan Hawkins, Innkeeper
Barnard Good House

3 cups all-purpose flour
1 tablespoon baking powder
1 tablespoon sugar
1 teaspoon baking soda
1 teaspoon salt
1½ cups buttermilk
½ cup sour cream or plain yogurt

Preheat oven to 350°.

Sift flour, baking powder, sugar, baking soda, and salt into a mixing bowl. Repeat twice. Add buttermilk and sour cream and mix well.

Form dough into a ball and transfer to a lightly floured surface (dough will be sticky). Roll dough into a 12 x 7 x 1-inch oval. Score top carefully and transfer to an ungreased baking sheet. Bake until loaf is brown, about 30 minutes.

YIELDS ONE LOAF

Habit Forming Cinnamon Buns

Anita and Karsten Dierk, Innkeepers
The Manse Bed and Breakfast Inn

1 cup milk
1 cup sugar
1 stick unsalted butter, softened
½ teaspoon salt (Sea salt is preferable.)
2 jumbo eggs
1 package fresh yeast
4 cups unbleached flour
2 tablespoons cinnamon
1 stick unsalted butter, melted
1 cup confectioners' sugar
½ cup heavy cream
½ tablespoon pure vanilla extract

Scald milk in a saucepan. Add ½ cup sugar, softened butter, and salt. Let mixture cool to lukewarm. Add eggs and fresh yeast. Mix well. Add 2 cups flour and beat well. Add remaining flour and mix well. (The dough will be sticky.) Refrigerate overnight.

When ready to continue, grease a large baking dish. Remove dough from refrigerator and divide in half. Place one half on a well-floured board or counter. Knead slightly, adding more flour if needed to keep dough from sticking. Roll dough into a rectangle as thin as possible without tearing.

Combine remaining ½ cup sugar and cinnamon. Spread dough with half of melted butter and half of sugar-cinnamon mixture. Roll dough carefully away from you, forming a cylinder. Pinch edge to seal. Cut buns by slicing cylinder into 2-inch sections. Place buns, cut side up, close together in baking dish so that buns look like pinwheels. Repeat process with remaining dough and filling. Cover with a tea towel and let buns rise at room temperature until doubled in size.

When ready to bake, preheat oven to 350°. Bake 20 to 25 minutes or until an inserted knife comes out clean. Combine confectioners' sugar, heavy cream, and vanilla extract. (This icing should be a bit runny.) Spread over warm buns and serve.

YIELDS APPROXIMATELY 12 LARGE BUNS

Strawberry Butter

Lorraine and Terry Schmidt, Owners/Innkeepers
The Humphrey Hughes House

1 cup unsalted butter, softened
2 tablespoons strawberry preserves
4 fresh strawberries, sliced

Place ingredients in a food processor and process until spreadable. Serve with pancakes, French toast, muffins, or scones, such as Cream Scones (Recipe appears on page 55.).

The Humphrey Hughes House

Innkeepers: Lorraine and Terry Schmidt
Favorite Foods: pasta and chocolate cake
Favorite Cape May Activity: dining in our fine restaurants

Blueberry Compote

Ed and Diane Hutchinson, Owners/Innkeepers
Fairthorne Bed & Breakfast

2 cups fresh or frozen blueberries
½ cup sugar
1 tablespoon cornstarch
Juice of ½ lemon

Place blueberries in a saucepan and cover with water. Cook slowly over medium heat. Combine sugar and cornstarch and mix completely. Before blueberries come to a boil, add sugar mixture to saucepan. Bring to a boil. Add lemon juice. Stir until thickened.

Serve over ice cream, pancakes, or French toast, such as French Toast Strata (Recipe appears on page 27.).

SERVES 8

Tea Time

Rum Raisin
Cheddar Spread
Cheese-Straw
Daisy Crackers
Butter Scones
Cream Scones with Strawberry Butter
Chocolate Cookies
Hamantaschen
Almond Macaroons
Coconut Macaroons
Ricotta Cheese Cookies
Strawberry Bars
Black Raspberry Almond Bars
Coffee Toffee Bars
Butter Finger Bars
Chocolate Praline Bars
Mom's Brownies
Frosted Peanut Butter Brownies
Decadent Candy
No Bake Chocolate-Topped Nut Chews
Velia's Coffee Cake
Cinnamon Coffee Cake
Russian Coffee Cake
Blueberry Coffee Cake
Orange Cranberry Bread
Banana Bread

Rum Raisin Cheddar Spread

Dane and Joan Wells, Innkeepers
The Queen Victoria® Bed and Breakfast

1 cup raisins
⅓ cup rum
6 ounces cream cheese, softened
8 ounces sharp Cheddar cheese, shredded

Soak raisins in rum for at least 1 hour.

Combine cream cheese and Cheddar cheese in a food processor and mix until smooth. Add raisins and rum and process briefly to slightly chop raisins. Chill well.

Serve with crackers, raw vegetables, or fruit wedges.

YIELDS 1½ CUPS

The Queen Victoria Bed and Breakfast

Web site: www.queenvictoria.com

Open: all year

Serves: breakfast and afternoon tea

Known for: warm hospitality and great attention to detail

Years in Business: 21

Cheese-Straw Daisy Crackers

**Tom and Sue Carroll, Innkeepers
The Mainstay Inn**

2 cups grated sharp Cheddar cheese, set aside to attain room temperature
½ cup butter
½ cup vegetable shortening
⅓ cup grated Romano cheese
1 tablespoon water
2 teaspoons salt
¼ teaspoon cayenne pepper
2 rounded cups all-purpose flour
1 teaspoon baking powder

Preheat oven to 375°.

In a food processor, cream Cheddar cheese, butter, shortening, Romano cheese, water, salt, and cayenne. Combine flour and baking powder and slowly mix into cheese mixture.

Place dough in a pastry bag with a large star tip and squeeze onto an ungreased baking sheet. Bake for 15 minutes or until crisp.

YIELDS 70 TO 80 DAISY CRACKERS

The Mainstay Inn

Web site: www.mainstayinn.com

Open: all year

Known for: stunning Victorian building

Most requested room: Bret Harte

Years in Business: 30

Butter Scones

Susan and Elan Zingman-Leith, Innkeepers
Leith Hall - Historic Seashore Inn

5 cups flour
1 tablespoon baking powder
2 teaspoons salt
10 tablespoons unsalted butter, cut into bits
½ cup golden raisins, dried cranberries, or currants
1½ cups cream or milk (We use cream.)
5 tablespoons sugar
1 egg, beaten

Preheat oven to 350°. Line cookie sheets with cooking parchment and spray with nonstick spray.

Sift together flour, baking powder, and salt. Blend in butter. Stir in fruit. Stir in cream and sugar.

Knead dough briefly. Pat out to ½-inch thick. Cut into triangles or 3-inch rounds. Glaze with beaten egg. Bake for 30 minutes or until golden. Serve with butter, jam, and marmalade.

Cream Scones
with Strawberry Butter

Lorraine and Terry Schmidt, Owners/Innkeepers
The Humphrey Hughes House

2 cups flour
2 teaspoons sugar
1 teaspoon salt
1 tablespoon baking powder
1 cup heavy cream
Strawberry Butter (Recipe appears on page 48.)

Preheat oven to 425°.

In a large bowl, sift together dry ingredients. Gradually add enough cream to form a soft dough. Knead lightly on a floured board, handling dough gently to retain air needed for scones to rise.

Roll out to a ½ to ¾-inch thickness.

Cut into 2-inch rounds and arrange on an ungreased baking sheet, leaving a ½-inch space between rounds. Bake for 10 to 12 minutes until golden brown. Serve with strawberry butter.

The Humphrey Hughes House

Web site: www.humphreyhugheshouse.com

Open: all year

Serves: breakfast and afternoon tea

Known for: spacious, gracious — excellent food!

Most requested room: all

Years in Business: 15

Chocolate Cookies

George and Kathleen Blinn, Innkeepers
Captain Mey's Bed & Breakfast Inn

½ cup shortening
½ cup butter
1 teaspoon vanilla
2½ cups flour
1 cup sugar
½ cup cocoa powder
½ teaspoon baking soda
¼ teaspoon salt
1 egg
2 tablespoons milk
Walnut or pecan halves

Beat together shortening and butter in a large bowl. Stir in vanilla.

In a separate bowl, mix together flour, sugar, cocoa, baking soda, and salt. Mix egg and milk together in a small cup.

Add dry ingredients to shortening mixture. Stir in egg mixture. If mixture is too dry, add more milk.

Shape dough into two balls. Chill for 2 hours.

Preheat oven to 375°. Reshape chilled dough into walnut-size balls. Place balls on an ungreased baking sheet and flatten with the bottom of a sugared glass. Press a walnut or pecan half into top of each cookie. Bake for 8 to 10 minutes.

YIELDS 5 DOZEN

Captain Mey's Bed & Breakfast Inn

Innkeepers: George and Kathleen Blinn

Favorite Foods: Italian

Favorite Cape May Activity: walking through Cape May's gaslit streets

Hamantaschen

Joe and JoAnne Tornambe, Innkeepers
Woodleigh House B&B

¼ pound butter
¼ pound margarine
1 cup sugar
¼ cup orange juice
4 cups flour
2 teaspoons baking pow der
3 eggs, beaten
Prune, apricot, or your favorite flavor preserves*
2 egg whites, beaten

Combine first 7 ingredients and mix well. Refrigerate dough for 1 hour.

Preheat oven to 350°. Roll out dough on a floured board. Using a small juice glass, cut dough into rounds. Place a dollop of preserves in center of each round. Moisten the edges, bring the sides together and pinch, forming a triangle. Brush with egg whites.

Bake for 20 to 30 minutes or until brown. Enjoy!

YIELDS ABOUT 3½ DOZEN

* Chopped nuts and raisins with a little cinnamon and sugar can be used instead of preserves.

Woodleigh House B&B

Innkeepers: Joe and JoAnne Tornambe

Favorite Foods: We like all types of food, especially unique ethnic dishes.

Favorite Cape May Activity: Joe is a runner. JoAnne likes walking the beach.

Almond Macaroons

Susan and Elan Zingman-Leith, Innkeepers
Leith Hall - Historic Seashore Inn

1 (8 ounces) can almond paste
1¼ cups sugar
2 egg whites

Preheat oven to 350°. Cover two cookie sheets with cooking parchment and spray with nonstick spray.

Break up almond paste into small pieces and place in a mixing bowl. Add sugar and egg whites. Beat with an electric mixer until fluffy.

Spoon into a large plastic food storage bag. Twist the top and cut off a corner. Bag is now a pastry cone.

Pipe 20 mounds on each cookie sheet. Bake for 20 minutes. Cool.

YIELDS 40 COOKIES

Leith Hall - Historic Seashore Inn

Innkeepers: Susan and Elan Zingman-Leith
Favorite Foods: chocolate anything, cream cheese pastries, French desserts
Favorite Cape May Activity: lying on the beach; touring other people's houses

Coconut Macaroons

Lenanne and James Labrusciano, Owners/Innkeepers
The Albert Stevens Inn

4 egg whites
2⅔ cups flaked coconut
⅔ cup sugar
6 tablespoons flour
¼ teaspoon salt
1 teaspoon almond extract

Preheat oven to 325°. Lightly grease a cookie sheet.

Beat egg whites until stiff. In a separate bowl, combine coconut, sugar, flour, and salt. Fold in egg whites and almond extract.

Drop by rounded teaspoonfuls onto prepared cookie sheet. Bake for 20 minutes or until edges are golden brown.

YIELDS 2 DOZEN

The Albert Stevens Inn

Web site: www.beachcomber.com/Capemay/Bbs/stevens.html

Open: all year

Serves: breakfast and afternoon tea

Known for: home of Dr. Albert Stevens, built in Queen Ann style

Most requested room: The Tower and The Study

Years in Business: 21

Ricotta Cheese Cookies

Robert Pasquarella, Chef
Angel of the Sea Bed & Breakfast

1 cup sugar
½ cup margarine, softened
1 egg
½ teaspoon vanilla
2 cups flour
½ teaspoon baking soda
1 cup ricotta cheese

Preheat oven to 350°.

Cream together sugar, margarine, and egg in a medium bowl. Add vanilla. Sift together flour and baking soda in a separate bowl. Add to creamed mixture. Stir in ricotta cheese.

Drop by tablespoonfuls onto a greased baking sheet. Bake for 10 to 12 minutes.

YIELDS 2½ DOZEN COOKIES

Strawberry Bars

Robert Pasquarella, Chef
Angel of the Sea Bed & Breakfast

3 cups flour
1½ cups chopped pecans
1½ cups butter, softened
1½ cups sugar
2 eggs
3 cups strawberry jam

Preheat oven to 350°. Lightly grease an 8 x 10-inch baking pan.

Combine all ingredients, except strawberry jam, in a medium-size bowl. Press three-quarters of mixture into prepared pan. Spread strawberry jam over mixture. Sprinkle remaining mixture over strawberry jam. Bake for 30 to 35 minutes or until golden brown. Let cool and cut into bars.

SERVES 8

Angel of the Sea Bed & Breakfast

Innkeepers: Gregory and Lorie Whissell
Favorite Foods: vegetarian dishes
Favorite Cape May Activity: shopping and going to the beach

Black Raspberry Almond Bars

Cindy and James Schmucker, Innkeepers
Bedford Inn

1 cup flour
¾ cup oats
½ cup sugar
½ cup butter, room temperature
½ teaspoon almond extract
½ cup black raspberry preserves
⅓ cup sliced almonds

Preheat oven to 350°. Spray an 8-inch square pan with nonstick spray.

Combine flour, oats, and sugar in a large bowl. Add butter and cut in with pastry blender or knives until mixture resembles coarse crumbs. Stir in almond extract until blended. Reserve about 1 cup mixture.

Press remaining mixture evenly over bottom of pan, adding more from reserve mixture if needed to cover. Spread preserves over top to about ½ inch from edges.

Mix almonds into reserved mixture. Sprinkle evenly over preserves and press down gently. (Some preserves will show through.) Bake for 25 to 30 minutes or until edges are golden. Cool in pan on wire rack. Cut into bars.

YIELDS 24 BARS

Coffee Toffee Bars

Sandra J. Miller, Owner/Innkeeper
Windward House Inn Bed and Breakfast

1 cup brown sugar, packed

½ cup butter

½ cup margarine

2 cups flour, lightly spooned into measuring cup and leveled off

2 tablespoons instant coffee

½ teaspoon baking powder

¼ teaspoon salt

1 teaspoon almond extract

1 cup chocolate chips

½ cup sliced almonds

1 cup confectioners' sugar

2 tablespoons butter, melted

1 to 2 tablespoons milk

1 teaspoon vanilla

Preheat oven to 350°. Grease a 10 x 15-inch jelly roll pan.

Beat together brown sugar, butter, and margarine until light and fluffy. Add flour, coffee, baking powder, salt, and almond extract to butter mixture. Blend well. (Dough will be crumbly.) Stir in chocolate chips and almonds.

Press dough evenly into prepared pan. Bake for 15 to 20 minutes. Combine remaining ingredients. Immediately spread over warm pastry. Cut into bars while still very warm. Chill before removing from pan.

YIELDS 2 DOZEN BARS

Windward House Inn

Innkeeper: Sandra J. Miller

Favorite Foods: Italian

Serves: brunch and afternoon tea

Favorite Cape May Activity: riding my bike, attending music festivals and local theater

Butter Finger Bars

Fred and Joan Echevarria, Innkeepers
Gingerbread House

1 cup butter, melted
½ cup granulated sugar
1 cup brown sugar, packed
4 cups oatmeal (not quick oats)
¾ cup peanut butter
1 cup chocolate chips

Preheat oven to 350°. Grease a 9 x 13-inch pan.

Mix together butter, sugars, and oatmeal. Pat mixture into pan. Bake for 15 minutes. Cool.

Melt together peanut butter and chocolate chips. Spread over cooled mixture. Cut into 2-inch-long bars.

YIELDS APPROXIMATELY 18 BARS

Gingerbread House

Web site: www.gingerbreadinn.com

Open: all year

Serves: brunch and afternoon tea

Known for: meticulously restored inn with magnificent woodworking craftsmanship and orginial paintings

Most requested room: Master Suite

Years in Business: 21

Chocolate Praline Bars

Robert Pasquarella, Chef
Angel of the Sea Bed & Breakfast

2 cups flour
1 cup plus ⅓ cup brown sugar, packed
½ cup plus ¾ cup butter
1 cup pecans
1 bag mini chocolate kisses or chocolate chips

Preheat oven to 350°. Lightly grease an 8 x 10-inch baking pan.

Mix flour and 1 cup brown sugar in a bowl. Cut in ½ cup butter until crumbly. Press mixture into prepared pan. Sprinkle pressed mixture with pecans. Reserve.

Combine remaining brown sugar and butter in a saucepan and heat over medium heat until boiling. Boil for 30 seconds. Pour mixture over pecans.

Bake for 13 to 18 minutes or until golden brown. Remove from oven and immediately sprinkle with chocolate kisses or chips. Let cool and cut into bars.

SERVES 8

Angel of the Sea Bed & Breakfast

Web site: www.angelofthesea.com

Open: all year

Serves: afternoon tea

Known for: architectural structure

Most requested room: Room #6

Years in Business: 12

Mom's Brownies

Susan and Elan Zingman-Leith, Innkeepers
Leith Hall - Historic Seashore Inn

6 ounces unsweetened chocolate
3 cups sugar
¾ cup oil
6 eggs
1 tablespoon vanilla extract
1 teaspoon salt
1½ cups all-purpose flour

Preheat oven to 350°. Line a jelly-roll pan with cooking parchment and spray with nonstick spray.

Melt chocolate and place in a mixing bowl. Beat in sugar, then oil, eggs, vanilla, salt, and finally flour.

Turn batter into pan. Smooth and bake for 27 minutes. Cool and cut into squares with a wet knife.

YIELDS 18 BROWNIES

Leith Hall - Historic Seashore Inn

Web site: www.leithhall.com

Open: all year

Serves: afternoon tea

Known for: ocean views and authentic Victorian interior

Most requested room: The Turkish Suite

Years in Business: 13

Frosted Peanut Butter Brownies

Lynda and Corbin Cogswell, Innkeepers
The Linda Lee Bed and Breakfast

1 cup plus ½ cup butter
⅓ cup plus ¼ cup cocoa
2 cups granulated sugar
1½ cups flour
½ teaspoon salt
4 large eggs
1 teaspoon vanilla
1 (18 ounces) jar chunky peanut butter
⅓ cup milk
10 large marshmallows or 100 mini-marshmallows
1 (16 ounces) box confectioners' sugar

Preheat oven to 350°. Grease a 15 x 10-inch jelly-roll pan.

Cook 1 cup butter and ⅓ cup cocoa over low heat until butter melts. Stir to combine and cool slightly. Combine sugar, flour, and salt in a large bowl. Add chocolate mixture and beat at medium speed until blended. Add eggs and vanilla and beat until just blended. Spread in prepared pan. Bake for 20 minutes or until a wooden pick inserted in the center comes out clean.

Remove lid from peanut butter and microwave peanut butter at 50% for 2 minutes, stirring once. Spread over warm brownies. Chill for 30 minutes.

Cook remaining ½ cup butter, milk, and marshmallows over low heat until marshmallows melt. Remove from heat and whisk in remaining ¼ cup cocoa. Gradually stir in confectioners' sugar until smooth. Spread over peanut butter. Chill for 20 minutes. Cut into squares.

YIELDS 6 DOZEN

Decadent Candy

Fred and Joan Echevarria, Innkeepers
Gingerbread House

1 sleeve saltine crackers
1 cup butter
1 cup brown sugar, packed
1½ cups mini chocolate chips
Chopped pecans, optional

Preheat oven to 350°. Spray a 10 x 15-inch cookie sheet with nonstick spray. Line sheet with tin foil and spray tin foil with nonstick spray.

Cover sheet with crackers. Melt butter and brown sugar over medium-high heat, stirring constantly until mixture comes to a boil. Pour over saltines. Bake for 15 minutes. Immediately sprinkle on chocolate chips and spread as they begin to melt. Sprinkle on pecans, if desired.

Refrigerate for a few hours. Remove from cookie sheet and break into uneven pieces.

Gingerbread House

Innkeepers: Fred and Joan Echevarria

Favorite Foods: afternoon tea

Favorite Cape May Activity: birding, tennis, and attending music festivals

No Bake Chocolate-Topped Nut Chews

Dane and Joan Wells, Innkeepers
The Queen Victoria® Bed and Breakfast

6 cups finely crushed vanilla wafers (about 90)

1 cup ground toasted almonds

1 cup butter, melted and cooled

½ cup sweetened condensed milk

¼ teaspoon salt

2 cups chocolate chips

Grease a rimmed 10 x 15-inch cookie pan.

Combine all ingredients, except chocolate chips, and mix well. Press into prepared pan.

Melt chocolate chips and stir until smooth. Spread over mixture. Chill until firm. Cut into 2 x 1-inch bars.

YIELDS 72 BARS

The Queen Victoria Bed and Breakfast

Innkeepers: Dane and Joan Wells

Favorite Foods: garlic mashed potatoes from
Waters Edge restaurant in Cape May

Favorite Cape May Activity: early morning walks on the
beachfront promenade

Velia's Coffee Cake

Kathy Mendolia and Sue Kulman, Innkeepers
Velia's Seaside Inn

1 cup sugar
¼ cup shortening
2 eggs, beaten
1½ cups plus 2 tablespoons flour
2 teaspoons baking powder
¼ teaspoon salt
½ cup milk
1 teaspoon vanilla extract
1 cup walnuts
1 cup brown sugar, packed
1 tablespoon cinnamon
2½ tablespoons butter, softened

Preheat oven to 350°. Grease a 9 x 11-inch glass cake pan.

Cream together sugar and shortening in a large bowl. Add eggs.

In a separate bowl, sift together 1½ cups flour, baking powder, and salt. Add flour mixture and milk alternately to wet mixture. Stir in vanilla. Spread half of batter into prepared pan.

Combine remaining flour, walnuts, brown sugar, and cinnamon. Cut in butter. Sprinkle half of walnut mixture over batter. Pour in remaining batter and smooth. Cover with remaining walnut mixture. Bake for 35 minutes.

SERVES 8 TO 10

Velia's Seaside Inn

Web site: www.veliasinn.com

Open: all year (almost)

Serves: breakfast and afternoon tea

Known for: restored Italianate Victorian with ocean views

Most requested room: Master Suite

Years in Business: 3

Cinnamon Coffee Cake

Kate Emerson, Owner/Innkeeper
Abigail Adams Bed & Breakfast By The Sea

½ cup butter, softened
1 cup plus ½ cup flour
1 cup sugar
1 tablespoon cinnamon
2 teaspoons baking powder
1 egg
½ cup milk

Preheat oven to 350°. Grease an 8 x 8-inch pan.

Mix together butter, 1 cup flour, sugar, and cinnamon. Reserve half of mixture.

Add remaining flour, baking powder, egg, and milk to remaining half of mixture. Pour into prepared pan. Sprinkle with reserved mixture. Bake for 30 minutes.

SERVES 8

Abigail Adams Bed & Breakfast by the Sea

Innkeeper: Kate Emerson
Favorite Foods: caramel pop corn
Favorite Cape May Activity: twilight walks along Cape May's gaslit streets

Russian Coffee Cake

Lucille and Dennis Doherty, Innkeepers
The Dormer House

2 teaspoons baking soda
2 cups sour cream
1 cup butter
2 cups plus ½ cup sugar
4 eggs
3 cups sifted flour
3 teaspoons baking powder
2 teaspoons vanilla
2 teaspoons cinnamon
4 tablespoons chopped nuts

Preheat oven to 350°. Grease and flour a 9 x 13-inch pan.

Add baking soda to sour cream and let stand. Cream together butter and 2 cups sugar. Add eggs and beat until smooth. Add in sour cream mixture. Stir in sifted flour and baking powder and beat until smooth. Add vanilla.

In a separate bowl, combine remaining sugar, cinnamon, and nuts.

Pour half of batter into pan. Cover with half the nut mixture. Repeat with remaining batter and nut mixture. Bake for 45 minutes. Let sit 30 minutes before serving. Enjoy!

SERVES 12 TO 15

The Dormer House

Web site: www.dormerhouse.com

Open: all year

Serves: breakfast and afternoon tea

Known for: glass enclosed breakfast porch with tables for two

Most requested room: Dormer Suite

Years in Business: 6

Blueberry Coffee Cake

Joe and Fran Geores, Innkeepers
The Inn at Journey's End

¼ cup butter or margarine
¾ cup sugar
1 egg
2 cups sifted all-purpose flour
2 teaspoons baking powder
½ teaspoon salt
½ cup milk
2 cups fresh blueberries, washed

Crumb Topping
¼ cup butter, softened
½ cup sugar
⅓ cup all-purpose flour
½ teaspoon cinnamon

Preheat oven to 375°. Grease a 9 x 9 x 2-inch pan.

Cream butter until fluffy. Add sugar and beat until light. Add egg and beat well.

Sift together dry ingredients. Add half the dry ingredients to butter mixture. Add ¼ cup milk and mix until well combined. Repeat with remaining dry ingredients and milk. Fold in berries. Pour into prepared pan.

Combine crumb topping ingredients and sprinkle over batter. Bake for 35 minutes.

SERVES 6 TO 9

The Inn at Journey's End

Innkeepers: Joe and Fran Geores

Favorite Cape May Activity: watching dolphins play under the setting sun; enjoying all of Cape May's wonderful restaurants

Orange Cranberry Bread

Don Schweikert, Innkeeper
Saltwood House Bed & Breakfast

2 sticks butter, softened
1 cup plus ½ cup sugar
4 eggs
2 tablespoons grated orange zest
1 teaspoon orange extract
2½ cups all-purpose flour
1 teaspoon baking powder
1 teaspoon baking soda
¼ teaspoon salt
1 cup plain yogurt
1 cup dried cranberries
½ cup orange juice

Preheat oven to 350°. Butter and flour two 8-inch loaf pans.

In a large mixing bowl, beat butter until fluffy. Beat in 1 cup sugar. Add eggs, one at a time, mixing well after each addition. Beat in orange zest and extract.

Sift together flour, baking powder, baking soda, and salt in a separate bowl. Fold one-third dry ingredients into wet ingredients. Mix in one-third yogurt. Repeat until all are combined. Add dried cranberries.

Pour into prepared loaf pans and bake for 50 to 60 minutes or until a toothpick inserted into the middle comes out clean.

While bread is baking, mix together remaining ½ cup sugar and orange juice in a small saucepan. Cook over medium heat until sugar dissolves, about 5 minutes.

When bread is done, remove from oven and pour hot syrup evenly over loaves. Let cool completely before unmolding.

SERVES 12 TO 16

Banana Bread

Elizabeth and Niels Favre, Innkeepers
Canterbury Cottage Inn B&B

2 cups sifted all-purpose flour
1 teaspoon baking soda
½ teaspoon salt
½ cup unsalted butter or margarine
1 cup sugar
2 eggs
1 cup mashed ripe bananas (about 2 bananas)
1 teaspoon fresh lemon juice
⅓ cup milk
½ cup chopped pecans

Preheat oven to 350°. Generously butter a 9 x 5 x 3-inch loaf pan.

Sift together flour, baking soda, and salt in a small bowl.

In a separate large bowl, cream butter until light. Gradually beat in sugar. Beat in eggs one at a time. Add mashed bananas and lemon juice and beat until well blended. Mix in dry ingredients, alternating with milk, beginning and ending with dry ingredients. Mix in pecans.

Pour batter into prepared pan and bake for about 1 hour and 20 minutes or until a cake tester comes out clean. Cool in pan for 10 minutes. Turn onto a rack and cool. Slice and serve.

YIELDS 12 SLICES

Canterbury Cottage Inn B&B

Innkeepers: Elizabeth and Niels Favre, Denise and Brian Favre

Favorite Foods: coffee cakes, Chinese and German foods

Favorite Cape May Activity: spending time with grandchildren

Social Hour

Party Food
Savory Crab Dip
Tapenade
Roasted Yellow Pepper Aïoli
Bruschetta Tomatoes
Tomato-Corn Salsa
Elegant Spinach Pie
Chinese Tortellini
Spinach and Artichokes in Puff Pastry
Three Sisters Quesadilla

Savory Crab Dip

Gregory Morrone, Head Chef
A Ca Mia

6 ounces goat cheese
½ cup sour cream
½ teaspoon Tabasco sauce
1 teaspoon black pepper
2 tablespoons lemon juice
1 pound lump crabmeat
½ cup fontina cheese
¼ cup chopped chives
Bruschetta Tomatoes (Recipe appears on page 81.)

Preheat oven to 450°. Grease six custard cups.

Combine goat cheese, sour cream, Tabasco, black pepper, and lemon juice in a food processor and process until smooth. Transfer to a mixing bowl. Carefully add crabmeat, fontina cheese, and chives.

Divide mixture evenly among custard cups and bake for 15 minutes or until nicely browned. Serve as is or top with bruschetta tomatoes.

SERVES 6

A Ca Mia

Web site: www.capemaydine.com

Open: seasonally

Serves: lunch and dinner

Menu: Northern Italian and contemporary American

Known for: outside patio and Euro-style dining

Years in business: 5

Tapenade

Executive Chef Mimi Wood
The Washington Inn

1 cup black olives
½ cup green olives
1 shallot, chopped
2 anchovy fillets, chopped
1 clove garlic, chopped
1 tablespoon capers
5 to 6 fresh basil leaves
1 tablespoon chopped parsley
2 tablespoons olive oil
1 tablespoon red wine vinegar
Dash of Tabasco sauce

Puree olives and shallot in a food processor. Remove. Place remaining ingredients in food processor and coarsely chop. Combine both mixtures in a bowl. Allow to sit at least 1 hour before serving.

Roasted Yellow Pepper Aïoli

Walter J. Jurusz, Executive Chef
The Pelican Club

1 yellow bell pepper
Olive oil
1 teaspoon chopped garlic
2 cups mayonnaise
1 tablespoon fresh squeezed lemon juice
Kosher salt to taste
Fresh cracked black pepper to taste
1 tablespoon hot sauce

Preheat oven to 400°.

Split yellow pepper in half and carefully clean out seeds. Lightly rub with olive oil. Place flat sides on a cookie sheet and bake until skin is black and blistery, about 20 to 30 minutes.

Immediately put pepper into an airtight container and refrigerate until cool. Peel skin off when cooled. Place roasted pepper and remaining ingredients in a food processor and puree until smooth. Chill before serving.

YIELDS 2 CUPS

The Pelican Club

Chef: Walter J. Jurusz

Chef's Training: graduated with honors 1998 from the Culinary Institute of America; also bachelor degrees in Econmics and History

Hobbies: surfing, travel

Favorite Foods: Spanish, South American, and Latin

Bruschetta Tomatoes

Gregory Morrone, Head Chef
A Ca Mia

2 large tomatoes, diced
¼ cup chopped basil
1 tablespoon minced garlic
3 tablespoons extra virgin olive oil
1 tablespoon balsamic vinegar
Pinch of salt and black pepper

Mix all ingredients in a bowl. Serve with grilled garlic bread as we do or with other flat bread.

SERVES 6

A Ca Mia

Chef: Gregory Morrone

Chef's Training: bachelor degree in Business Law; has worked in restaurants since 1975

Favorite Foods: wild boar Bolognese

Tomato-Corn Salsa

Anita and Karsten Dierk, Innkeepers
The Manse Bed and Breakfast Inn

3 to 4 large ears fresh corn
7 to 8 large fresh tomatoes
1 red onion, diced
Generous handful chopped cilantro
Sea salt to taste (at least 2 teaspoons)
Juice of 6 or 7 limes (more if limes are small)
Fresh herbs (sprigs of rosemary, sage, thyme, oregano, marjoram, or
   whatever suits your fancy)

Husk corn. Cook in boiling water to desired doneness, approximately 5 to
10 minutes. Cool slightly and remove kernels from cobs. Cut tomatoes into
a semi-fine dice (a little smaller than the size of a sugar cube).

   Combine corn, tomatoes, and remaining ingredients, except herbs, and
mix well. Garnish with fresh herbs. Serve with a frittata, corn chips, or
fresh fried fish.

The Manse Bed and Breakfast Inn

Web site: www.themanse.com

Open: all year

Serves: breakfast and afternoon tea

Known for: great food, owner occupant hospitality

Most requested room: 2 or 3

Years in Business: 20

Elegant Spinach Pie

Toby and Andy Fontaine, Innkeepers
Bayberry Inn

2 (10 ounces) packages frozen spinach
3 tablespoons olive oil
2 medium onions, finely chopped
8 ounces mushrooms, sliced
½ medium red bell pepper, chopped
4 eggs
1½ cups grated Parmesan cheese
1 cup ricotta cheese
Salt and pepper to taste
Pie dough for 10-inch double crust pie

Preheat oven to 425°.

Cook spinach according to package directions. Drain and press out liquid.

Heat oil in a 10-inch skillet over medium heat. Add onions and cook gently for about 5 minutes. Add mushrooms and peppers in the last 2 minutes.

In a large bowl, beat eggs until foamy. Add spinach and onion mixture to eggs. Add Parmesan, ricotta, and salt and pepper.

Divide pie dough in half. Roll each into a round. Line a 10-inch pie plate with one crust round. Fill with spinach mixture. Cover with second round. Seal and flute edges. Cut vents in top.

Bake on a rack below center of oven for about 40 minutes or until golden. Let stand on a wire rack for 10 minutes before serving.

SERVES 8

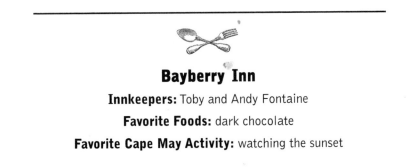

Bayberry Inn

Innkeepers: Toby and Andy Fontaine
Favorite Foods: dark chocolate
Favorite Cape May Activity: watching the sunset

Chinese Tortellini

Cynthia and Tom Riker, Innkeepers
The Puffin

13 to 16 ounces frozen tortellini
4 tablespoons soy sauce
4 teaspoons sesame oil
⅓ cup sesame seeds
Chopped green onions, optional

Cook tortellini according to package directions. Drain well.

Cover a cookie sheet with foil wrap. Place tortellini on tray. Toss with soy sauce and sesame oil. Sprinkle with sesame seeds. Marinate for at least 2 hours or overnight in refrigerator.

When ready to serve, preheat oven to 400°. Bake for 15 minutes. Sprinkle with green onion. Serve with toothpicks.

SERVES 10 TO 12

The Puffin

Innkeepers: Cynthia and Tom Riker

Favorite Foods: lobster and ice cream

Favorite Cape May Activity: relaxing on the porch and enjoying the ambiance of Jackson Street; having the beach only a half block away

Spinach and Artichokes in Puff Pastry

Lynda and Corbin Cogswell, Innkeepers
The Linda Lee Bed and Breakfast

1 package frozen puff pastry (Pepperidge Farms is fine.)
10 ounces frozen chopped spinach, thawed
14 ounces artichoke hearts, drained and chopped
½ cup mayonnaise
½ cup grated Parmesan cheese
1 teaspoon onion powder
1 teaspoon garlic powder
½ teaspoon pepper

Thaw puff pastry at room temperature for 30 minutes.

Meanwhile, drain spinach well and press spinach between layers of paper towel. Combine spinach and remaining ingredients.

Unfold one pastry sheet and place on a lightly floured surface or heavy duty plastic wrap. Spread one-quarter spinach mixture evenly over pastry sheet, leaving a ½-inch border. Roll pastry, jelly-roll fashion, pressing to seal seam. Wrap in heavy duty plastic wrap. Repeat with remaining pastry and spinach mixture. Freeze for 30 minutes.

Preheat oven to 400°. Remove rolls from freezer. Cut into ½-inch-thick slices. Bake for 20 minutes or until golden brown.

YIELDS 4 DOZEN SLICES

The Linda Lee Bed and Breakfast

Innkeepers: Lynda and Corbin Cogswell

Favorite Cape May Activity: enjoying the unique architectural styles and the many cultural offerings

Three Sisters Quesadilla

Randy and Susi Bithell, Chef/Owners
Gecko's

Canola oil
2 cobs fresh corn, fire roasted or 8 ounces frozen corn, oven roasted
8 ounces lima beans, cooked
1 medium summer squash, diced
1 small red onion, finely diced
1 small or medium jalapeño, finely diced
Salt and pepper
8 large flour tortillas
8 ounces Jack or slightly sharp Cheddar cheese, shredded
Chopped fresh cilantro
Sour cream, optional
Guacamole, optional
Salsa or pico de gallo, optional

Heat a sauté or frying pan over medium-high heat. Drizzle a little canola oil in pan. When hot, add roasted corn kernels, lima beans, squash, onion, and jalapeño. Cook only until squash begins to soften and all ingredients are hot. Salt and pepper to taste.

Place a heavy pan or griddle over medium-low heat. (I like to use cast iron.) Place a tortilla in pan. Cover with a thin layer of cheese. Add one-quarter vegetable mixture, spreading out evenly. Sprinkle with cilantro and cover with another tortilla. When cheese begins to melt and tortilla is

---

Gecko's

Web site: www.capemaydine.com

Open: seasonally

Serves: lunch, dinner, and brunch

Menu: Southwestern

Known for: casual indoor and outdoor seating

Years in business: 2

browned, carefully turn with a metal spatula and cook until golden. (Lower the flame if the tortilla cooks faster than the cheese melts.)

Transfer quesadilla to a cutting board and cut into wedges. Hold in warm oven until ready to serve. Repeat process three more times with remaining tortillas and ingredients.

Serve with sour cream, guacamole, and your preferred salsa or, better yet, fresh-made pico de gallo.

SERVES 4

Starters,
Soups &
Salads

Roasted Stuffed Pepper

Marinated Tomatoes

Mussels Mekong

Mussels in Tomato-Basil Gorgonzola Broth

Escargot in Garlic Cream

Peppered Ahi Tuna with Black Bean Sauce

Field Green Salad with Toasted Pumpkin Seed Vinaigrette

Heirloom Tomato Salad

Warm Escarole Salad

Coconut Orange Vinaigrette

Cold Cranberry Soup

Lucille's Onion Soup

Lobster Bisque

Cioppino Broth

Roasted Stuffed Pepper

Mimi Wood, Executive Chef
The Washington Inn

½ cup balsamic vinegar
4 red or yellow bell peppers, tops cut off
8 slices fontina cheese
8 tablespoons goat cheese
4 thin slices prosciutto ham, chopped
8 tablespoons Tapenade (Recipe appears on page 79.)
4 tablespoons Marinated Tomatoes (see recipe)
2 cups mixed greens

Heat balsamic vinegar in a saucepan over low heat until liquid is reduced by half. Cool.

Meanwhile, place peppers under a hot preheated broiler, turning until blackened. Place blackened peppers in a brown bag and close tightly or in a bowl covered with a plate. Let sit for a few minutes. (The steam loosens the skins for easy peeling.) When peppers are cool enough to handle, pull off skins. Do not rinse. Cut out stems and seeds.

Reduce oven temperature to 375°. Stuff each pepper with 2 slices fontina cheese, 2 tablespoons goat cheese, one-quarter chopped ham, 2 tablespoons tapenade, and 1 tablespoon tomatoes. Place in a shallow baking dish, open sides up, and bake for 15 to 20 minutes. Divide greens between 4 plates and top with a pepper. Drizzle with vinegar and serve.

SERVES 4

The Washington Inn

Web site: www.washingtoninn.com

Open: February through December

Cuisine: contemporary American

Serves: dinner, on and off-premise catering

Known for: elegant atmosphere, award-winning food, huge wine cellar

Years in Business: 24

Marinated Tomatoes

Executive Chef Mimi Wood
The Washington Inn

2 cups chopped very ripe tomatoes
¼ cup olive oil
2 tablespoons balsamic vinegar
1 tablespoon chopped garlic
2 tablespoons thinly sliced fresh basil
¼ teaspoon salt
Fresh ground black pepper

Mix together all ingredients. Marinate at room temperature for a few hours.

Mussels Mekong

George Pechin, Chef/Owner
Peaches at Sunset

2 tablespoons vegetable oil
1 heaping tablespoon red curry paste
3 (8 ounces) cans unsweetened coconut milk
2 tablespoons fish sauce
3 tablespoons sugar
4 dozen frozen Kiwi mussels, thawed or fresh cleaned, debearded mussels
½ bunch fresh cilantro, chopped
½ bunch fresh basil, chopped

Heat vegetable oil in a saucepan over medium-high heat. Add curry paste and fry for about 2 minutes. Add 1 can coconut milk and whisk well. Bring to a boil. Add remaining milk and return to a boil. Reduce heat and simmer for approximately 20 minutes.

Add fish sauce and sugar. (Add more sauce or sugar depending on your taste preference. Fish sauce will make it saltier, and sugar will cut down on the spiciness.) Keep warm until ready to serve.

Place mussels and 1 to 2 cups water in a pot over medium-high heat. Simmer until all mussels are open, approximately 5 to 10 minutes. (If using Kiwi mussels, simply steam as they are on the half shell.) Drain and place in a serving bowl.

Add cilantro and basil to sauce and stir to combine. Pour over mussels.

SERVES 4 TO 6

Peaches at Sunset

Chef: George Pechin

Chef's Training: one year at the Culinary Institute of America and apprenticeships in several Philadelphia restaurants

Hobbies: travel; being in the business for 20 years

Favorite Foods: Thai and Mexican foods

Mussels in Tomato-Basil Gorgonzola Broth

Walter J. Jurusz, Executive Chef
The Pelican Club

6 tablespoons pure olive oil
2 tablespoons minced garlic
4 pounds Prince Edward Island mussels, cleaned
1 to 2 cups white wine
Kosher salt to taste
Cracker black pepper to taste
4 to 8 cups San Marzano Tomato Sauce (Recipe appears on page 133.)
½ cup crumbled Gorgonzola cheese
¼ cup thinly sliced fresh basil
1 pound fresh fettuccini or linguine, optional

Heat oil over medium heat in a large skillet. Lightly sauté garlic. (Do not brown.) Add mussels and stir to coat with oil. Add white wine and simmer for 20 seconds. Add salt and pepper. Add San Marzano tomato sauce, cheese, and basil. Simmer until all mussels are open, approximately 5 to 10 minutes.

Pour into serving bowls or over pasta. Serve with your favorite crusty bread for dipping and enjoying.

SERVES 4

Escargot in Garlic Cream

Neil R. Elsohn, Executive Chef/Owner
Waters Edge Restaurant

2 ounces clarified butter
2 cups quartered mushrooms
24 large escargot
2 teaspoons minced garlic
Juice of 1 lemon
½ cup dry white wine
12 ounces heavy cream
Salt and white pepper to taste
1 tablespoon chopped parsley or chives
Toast points or puff pastry

Melt butter in a large skillet over medium heat. Add mushrooms and sauté until slightly softened. Add escargot, garlic, lemon juice, and wine. Cook until liquid is reduced by two-thirds.

Add heavy cream and salt and pepper. Reduce to a sauce-like consistency. Add parsley or chives. Serve immediately on toast points or in puff pastry.

SERVES 4

Waters Edge Restaurant

Web site: www.watersedgerestaurant.com

Cuisine: gourmet American

Open: all year **Serves:** dinner and drinks

Known for: fabulous food

Years in Business: 15

Peppered Ahi Tuna with Black Bean Sauce

Harry Gleason, Chef/Owner
Daniel's on Broadway

1 pound sushi grade tuna
¼ cup coarse ground black pepper
¼ cup sesame oil
½ cup canned black beans, drained (reserve some liquid)
3 tablespoons sherry
1 tablespoon sugar
2 tablespoons chopped garlic
Salt and white pepper to taste
Vegetable Confetti (Recipe appears on page 127.)
Pickled ginger, sliced
Soy sauce
Wasabi paste

Roll tuna liberally in pepper. Heat oil in a sauté pan over high heat. Add tuna and sear briefly on all sides. Refrigerate.

Place beans, sherry, sugar, garlic, and salt and white pepper in a blender and puree until smooth. (Sauce should be pourable but not runny. If too thick, add some reserved liquid from beans.) Refrigerate.

Cut tuna into ⅛-inch-thick slices. Divide into four portions and arrange along one side of four chilled plates. Spoon sauce on other side of plates. Place vegetable confetti in center of plates. Garnish with pickled ginger, a small ramekin of soy sauce, and a dollop of wasabi paste.

SERVES 4

Field Green Salad with Toasted Pumpkin Seed Vinaigrette

Neil R. Elsohn, Executive Chef/Owner
Waters Edge Restaurant

¼ cup pumpkin seeds, toasted
¼ cup rice wine vinegar
Juice of 1 lime
¾ cup extra virgin olive oil
Coarse salt and freshly cracked pepper to taste
6 cups field greens
6 ounces "Coach Farm" goat cheese
1½ cups chopped mixed tropical fruits (mango, papaya, star fruit,
    pineapple, or your choice)

Puree pumpkin seeds, vinegar, and lime juice in a processor. Slowly drizzle
in olive oil. Season to taste with salt and pepper. Toss vinaigrette with
remaining ingredients. Eat!

SERVES 4

Waters Edge Restaurant

Chef: Neil E. Elshon, Executive Chef; Glenn Turner, Chef

Chef's Training: mama; The New York Restaurant School;
eating out a lot

Hobbies: too many to list

Favorite Foods: foie gras, potato pancakes, smoked salmon,
scallions

Heirloom Tomato Salad

Andrew J. Carthy, Chef
The Ebbitt Room at The Virginia Hotel

2 tablespoons white balsamic vinegar

4 to 5 heirloom tomatoes, washed and sliced

½ medium red onion, julienned

½ head fennel, sliced paper thin

1 tablespoon chopped basil

2 to 3 tablespoons lemon oil

Salt and pepper

1 cup ricotta salata, cut into cubes

4 cups mixed greens

1½ tablespoons basil oil

1 hothouse cucumber, sliced into paper thin discs

Cook white balsamic vinegar over medium-high heat until reduced by half. Do not burn. Cool.

Combine cooled vinegar, tomatoes, onion, fennel, basil, and lemon oil in a large bowl. Season with salt and pepper. Add ricotta salata. In a separate bowl, toss greens with basil oil. Season with salt and pepper.

Arrange cucumber slices in a circle on four glass salad plates. Place tomato salad in center and top with mixed greens. Drizzle with additional basil oil, balsamic reduction, and lemon oil, if you like.

SERVES 4

The Ebbitt Room at The Virginia Hotel

Web site: www.virginiahotel.com

Cuisine: New American

Open: all year   **Serves:** dinner

Known for: excellent food, atmosphere, service, and romance

Most requested table: Table 1

Years in Business: 12

Warm Escarole Salad

Neil R. Elsohn, Executive Chef/Owner
Waters Edge Restaurant

½ cup rice wine vinegar
½ cup extra virgin olive oil
2 tablespoons crushed garlic (or more to taste)
1 teaspoon salt
½ teaspoon white pepper
6 cups escarole leaves, cleaned

Combine all ingredients, except escarole, in a pot and bring to a boil. Add escarole. Toss briefly and cook for 30 to 45 seconds. Serve immediately.

SERVES 4

Coconut Orange Vinaigrette

Mimi Wood, Executive Chef
The Washington Inn

1 cup orange juice concentrate
¼ cup water
7 ounces coconut milk
Juice of 1 lime
2 tablespoons honey
1 tablespoon chopped shallots
2 cups olive oil
¼ cup toasted coconut
1 tablespoon pink peppercorns
Pinch of cayenne pepper
Salt and white pepper to taste

Combine orange juice concentrate, water, coconut milk, lime juice, honey, and shallots. Using a whisk or hand blender, slowly add olive oil. Add toasted coconut, pink peppercorns, and cayenne pepper. Season to taste with salt and white pepper.

WILL DRESS 6 SALADS

The Washington Inn

Chef: Mimi Wood

Chef's Training: on the job at restaurants in California, Caribbean, Switzerland, and New England

Accomplishments: voted 1997 Best Chef in South Jersey; assisted in writing "The Washington Inn Cooks for Friends"

Favorite Foods: Italian influenced

Cold Cranberry Soup

Nan Hawkins, Innkeeper
Barnard Good House

6 cups fresh cranberries
4 cups water
2 whole cloves, tied in cheesecloth bag
1½ cups sugar
4½ teaspoons all-purpose flour
2¼ cups sour cream or yogurt
1½ cups dry red wine*
1½ cups *fresh* orange juice
Sour cream
Fresh mint sprigs

Simmer cranberries, water, and cloves in a large saucepan for 10 minutes. Drain cranberries, reserving 1 cup liquid. Discard cloves. Puree cranberries in a blender. Press through a strainer into a heavy large saucepan. Mix in reserved cooking liquid.

Combine sugar and flour in a medium bowl. Stir in 2¼ cups sour cream, wine, and orange juice. Mix into cranberries. Slowly bring to boil, stirring constantly. Reduce heat and simmer for 2 minutes, stirring constantly. Cool and refrigerate until well chilled. (This soup can be prepared 1 day in advance.)

Garnish with sour cream and mint sprigs.

SERVES 10 TO 12

* Sometimes I also add a bit of cranberry liqueur to enhance the flavor.

Barnard Good House

Innkeeper: Nan Hawkins

Favorite Foods: almost everything

Favorite Cape May Activity: swimming and entertaining guests

Lucille's Onion Soup

Dot Burton and Lucille Thompson, Chefs
The Chalfonte Hotel

4 cups thinly sliced, large mild onions
5 tablespoons butter or margarine
¼ teaspoon pepper
5⅓ cups chicken stock
5 beef bouillon cubes (dissolved in 1 cup boiling water)
1 teaspoon salt
5 (2 inches) toast rounds
Garlic butter
Parmesan cheese, optional

In a large pot, sauté onions in butter until golden brown. Sprinkle with pepper. Add stock, beef broth, and salt. Cover and simmer for about 1 hour. (If there's time, let the soup sit overnight to enhance the flavor.)

Lightly spread toast rounds with garlic butter and broil until brown. Place a toast round in each bowl and cover with soup. If desired, sprinkle with parmesan cheese.

SERVES 5

Lobster Bisque

Mimi Wood, Executive Chef
The Washington Inn

2 cups diced onions
1 cup diced celery
1 cup diced carrots
1 bunch fresh thyme, chopped
1 teaspoon chopped fresh garlic
1 bay leaf
½ cup butter
½ cup flour
½ cup brandy
6 cups lobster stock or lobster base
1 tablespoon tomato paste
Pinch of cayenne pepper
1 teaspoon Worcestershire sauce
2 cups heavy cream
½ to 1 pound lobster meat
Salt and white pepper

Sauté onions, celery, carrots, thyme, garlic, and bay leaf in butter until onions are golden brown. Add flour and stir well. Cook for a few minutes until a nice paste forms. Add brandy, lobster stock, tomato paste, cayenne pepper, and Worcestershire sauce. Whisk until thick and smooth. Simmer for 30 minutes.

Strain broth and return to pan. Add cream and lobster meat and cook until warmed through. Season with salt and white pepper to taste.

SERVES 8

Cioppino Broth

Richard Walter, Executive Chef
Aleathea's at The Inn of Cape May

1 tablespoon olive oil
4 cloves garlic, chopped
2 tablespoons chopped shallots
1 cup peeled, seeded, and chopped tomatoes
1 tablespoon tomato paste
½ cup white wine
2 cups chicken stock
1 cup clam juice
1 tablespoon fresh thyme
8 ounces shiitake mushrooms, trimmed and halved
½ bunch basil, cut into thin strips

Heat olive oil in a medium saucepan over medium heat. Add garlic, shallots, and chopped tomatoes. Cook for about 5 minutes. Add tomato paste and cook briefly. Add wine. Stir and cook until liquid is noticeably reduced.

Add chicken stock and clam juice. Bring to a boil, then reduce heat and simmer for a few minutes. Add fresh thyme and simmer for 2 minutes. Remove from heat. Stir in shiitake mushrooms and basil.

SERVES 4

Aleathea's

Web site: www.aleatheas.com

Cuisine: New American with an emphasis on seafood, steaks, and chops

Open: 10 months a year **Serves:** lunch, dinner, and drinks

Known for: beach front dining with ocean breezes in a Victorian setting

Most requested table: porch

Years in Business: 16

Entrees

Herb Chicken

Chicken Mascarpone

Pan-Roasted Duck Breast with Crispy Herb Risotto Cake

Cape Fillet of Beef

Roasted Fillet of Beef with Blue Cheese-Horseradish Cream

Braised Lamb Shank with Dark Rum and Root Veggies

Tuna with Honey Mustard Ginger Sauce

Hazelnut Vanilla Crusted Halibut with Coconut Orange Vinaigrette

Grouper Charleston

Lacquered Sea Bass in Cioppino Broth

Chilean Sea Bass Papillotte with Tomato Reduction

Flounder Francaise with Sweet Lemon Sauce

Pelican Club Crab Cakes

Farfalle with Smoked Salmon and Asparagus

Lobster Pasta

Veggie Burgers

Grilled Veggie Hoagies

Herb Chicken

Barbara Bray Wilde, Innkeeper
The Southern Mansion Bed & Breakfast

2 (8 ounces) boneless chicken breasts, skin removed
1 cup grated sharp provolone
2 large roasted peppers, sliced into strips
4 tablespoons dried herbs of your choice
½ cup heavy cream
2 tablespoons butter
2 tablespoons white wine
½ teaspoon minced garlic
Salt and pepper to taste

Preheat oven to 350°. Lightly grease a baking sheet.

Cut chicken breasts in half horizonally and pound flat. Spread cheese over chicken. Cover with roasted pepper. Roll chicken into tight cylinders and coat with herbs. Place on sheet and bake for 25 minutes or until cooked through.

Meanwhile, combine remaining ingredients in a saucepan over medium-high heat. Cook until liquid is reduced by three-quarters.

Slice chicken, place on serving plates, and drape with sauce.

SERVES 4

The Southern Mansion Bed & Breakfast

Web site: www.southernmansion.net

Open: all year

Serves: breakfast, afternoon tea, and dinner with room packages

Known for: gardens, architectural structure, large bedrooms

Most requested room: Master Suite - 750 square feet

Years in Business: 6

Chicken Mascarpone

Ed Henry, Owner
Henry's on the Beach

1 pound mascarpone cheese
½ pound Parmesan cheese, grated
½ cup pesto
¼ pound crab meat
3 large shrimp, peeled, deveined, and finely chopped
6 eggs
Salt and pepper to taste
8 (7 ounces) chicken breasts, boneless, skinless, and evenly tenderized
½ cup Japanese breadcrumbs

Combine mascarpone, Parmesan, pesto, crab meat, shrimp, and 2 eggs. Season with salt and pepper.

Slice each chicken breast lengthwise to form a pocket. Fill pockets with mascarpone mixture. Seal well.

Lightly whisk remaining 4 eggs. Dip breasts in egg wash. Cover with breadcrumbs. Place on a baking sheet and refrigerate for 2 hours.

When ready to serve, preheat oven to 375°. Bake for 30 to 40 minutes until well browned.

SERVES 8

Henry's on the Beach

Cuisine: lots of seafood

Open: seasonally **Serves:** lunch, dinner, and brunch

Known for: ocean front deck and family friendly

Most requested table: perimeter tables on the deck

Years in Business: 4

Pan-Roasted Duck Breast with Crispy Herb Risotto Cake

Harry Gleason, Chef/Owner
Daniel's on Broadway

6 tablespoons olive oil
6 boneless duck breast halves
Salt and pepper to taste
6 cups prepared risotto
¾ cup grated Parmesan cheese
1 tablespoon chopped chives
1 tablespoon rosemary
1 tablespoon thyme
1 large egg, beaten
¾ cup seasoned breadcrumbs
3 tablespoons chopped shallots
½ cup balsamic vinegar
½ cup fresh orange juice
5 tablespoons cold butter, diced
½ cup red wine

Preheat oven to 400°. Heat 2 tablespoons olive oil in a large pan over medium heat. Season duck breasts with salt and pepper and brown, skin

---

Daniel's on Broadway

Web site: www.danielscapemay.com

Cuisine: American Continental with ethnic touches

Open: all year **Serves:** brunch and dinner

Known for: great food, intimate dining rooms, 1713-era house, and beautiful landscaping

Most requested table: It's a secret.

Years in Business: 5

side down, for 10 minutes. Turn and continue to brown for 2 to 3 minutes. Place duck on a baking sheet and bake in oven for 5 minutes. Pour off all but 1 tablespoon oil from browning pan. Reserve tablespoon in pan.

In a large bowl, combine risotto, Parmesan cheese, herbs, and egg. Evenly divide mixture and shape into 6 cakes. Dredge in seasoned breadcrumbs.

In a second pan, heat remaining 4 tablespoons oil over medium heat. Brown cakes for 2 to 3 minutes on each side. Keep warm.

In first pan, sauté shallots until softened, about 2 to 3 minutes. Add vinegar and reduce over high heat, about 1 to 2 minutes. Add orange juice, simmer until slightly thickened. Add butter, one piece at a time, until completely dissolved and sauce has a smooth consistency.

Slice each duck breast. Place a risotto cake on each of six large plates. Fan the duck breast around each cake and drizzle with sauce.

SERVES 6

Cape Fillet of Beef

Barbara Bray Wilde, Innkeeper
The Southern Mansion Bed & Breakfast

Butter or olive oil
4 (8 ounces) beef tenderloins
12 shiitake mushrooms
2 teaspoons minced garlic
10 strands fresh thyme
8 sage leaves
2 sprigs rosemary
1 teaspoon black pepper
4 tablespoons red balsamic vinegar
4 tablespoons Merlot wine
Beef stock
1 cup demi-glace (available in most supermarkets or gourmet stores)

Heat a large sauté pan over medium-high heat. Add enough butter or oil to coat pan. Add beef and brown on each side.

Add mushrooms, garlic, and herbs. Add vinegar and wine. If liquid dries too quickly, add a little beef stock. Cook until desired doneness.

Remove herbs. Stir in demi-glace. Serve beef covered in sauce.

SERVES 4

Roasted Fillet of Beef with Blue Cheese-Horseradish Cream

Mimi Wood, Executive Chef
The Washington Inn

½ cup mayonnaise
½ cup sour cream
1½ tablespoons horseradish
1¼ cups crumbled blue cheese
Juice of ½ lemon
1 teaspoon Worcestershire sauce
Salt and fresh pepper
1 whole (5 to 6 pounds) tenderloin, unpeeled
1 cup Dijon mustard

Combine first 6 ingredients. Season to taste with salt and pepper. Let flavors marry for approximately 2 hours.

Preheat oven to 500°. Trim silverskin and excess fat off tenderloin. (For the easiest solution, ask your butcher to make the fillet oven-ready.) Season with salt and pepper. Rub Dijon mustard over entire tenderloin. Roast in a baking pan for 35 to 40 minutes until medium rare to medium.

Let sit before serving. Slice fillet into 1-inch-thick slices. Shingle slices on a cutting board or serving platter. Place blue cheese-horseradish cream in a small bowl and serve on the side for dipping.

SERVES 10 TO 12

Braised Lamb Shank with Dark Rum and Root Veggies

Neil R. Elsohn, Executive Chef/Owner
Waters Edge Restaurant

4 ancho chiles
Vegetable oil
Coarse salt and freshly cracked pepper
4 lamb shanks (about 12 to 14 ounces each)
2 tablespoon olive oil
2 medium onions, cubed
2 carrots, peeled and cubed
1 celery root, cubed
3 parsnips, peeled and cubed
1 mango, cubed
1 cup brown sugar, packed
1 cup Meyers rum
2 tablespoons orange juice concentrate
1½ quarts chicken stock

Preheat oven to 325°. Rehydrate chiles in warm water until soft. Squeeze out extra water and reserve.

Coat a large ovenproof skillet or Dutch oven with oil and heat over medium-high heat. Generously salt and pepper lamb shanks. Place shanks in skillet and brown on all sides. Remove shanks from skillet and pour off oil. Add olive oil, onions, carrots, celery root, and parsnips and sauté briefly.

Add chiles, shanks, and remaining ingredients and bring to a boil.

Cover loosely and bake in oven for 2 to 2½ hours or until meat is very tender and beginning to fall off the bone.

SERVES 4

Tuna with Honey Mustard Ginger Sauce

George Pechin, Chef/Owner
Peaches at Sunset

1 quart heavy cream
1 2-inch piece ginger, peeled and julienned
3 tablespoons Dijon mustard
2 tablespoons honey
Salt and pepper to taste
4 (8 to 10 ounces) pieces tuna
Vegetable or olive oil

Combine cream and ginger in a saucepan and bring to a boil. Reduce heat and simmer, stirring occasionally with a wooden spoon until sauce reduces by at least half. Remove from heat and strain sauce. Add Dijon mustard, honey, and salt and pepper.

Season tuna with oil and salt and pepper. Cook tuna on a hot grill or in a sauté pan for about 3 minutes per side or to desired doneness (should be red or pink inside).

Divide sauce between 4 plates and top with tuna.

SERVES 4

Peaches at Sunset
Cuisine: Pacific Rim
Open: all year **Serves:** dinner
Known for: eclectic cuisine with Asian influence
Most requested table: booth by the fish tank
Years in Business: 20

Hazelnut Vanilla Crusted Halibut with Coconut Orange Vinaigrette

Mimi Wood, Executive Chef
The Washington Inn

¾ cup hazelnuts
1 cup Japanese breadcrumbs
2 teaspoons grated ginger
1 teaspoon vanilla bean powder
12 tablespoons unsalted butter, softened
Salt to taste
Pinch of cayenne pepper
6 (8 ounces) halibut fillets
White pepper
Soy oil
1 or 2 tablespoons butter
Coconut Orange Vinaigrette (Recipe appears on page 99.)

Toast hazelnuts in a toaster oven until golden brown. Cool.

Place nuts in a food processor and pulse until finely chopped. Combine nuts with breadcrumbs, ginger, and vanilla bean powder. Cut butter into crumb mixture. Season with salt and cayenne pepper.

Preheat oven to 375°. Season fillets with salt and white pepper. Heat sauté pan over medium-high heat. Coat pan with oil. Add butter. (You'll know the pan is hot enough if butter browns quickly.) Add fillets and sear each side until nicely browned.

Transfer fillets to an ovenproof pan. Top each fillet with crumb mixture. Bake for 15 to 20 minutes. Serve with coconut orange vinaigrette.

SERVES 6

Grouper Charleston

Harry Gleason, Chef/Owner
Daniel's on Broadway

½ cup butter

4 (8 ounces) grouper fillets, skin off and center bones removed

½ cup flour

1½ cups julienned leeks

1½ cups fresh sweet white corn kernels

1½ cups diced fresh tomatoes

1 cup sherry

1 cup lobster stock

1½ cups heavy cream

Salt and white pepper to taste

8 ounces lobster meat, coarsely chopped

4 tablespoons finely chopped parsley

Preheat oven to 450°. Melt butter in a large sauté pan over medium heat. Dredge fillets in flour, shaking off excess. Lightly brown for about 2 minutes per side. Remove fillets from pan and place on a nonstick baking sheet. Bake for 7 to 10 minutes.

Place leeks, corn, and tomatoes in same pan in which grouper fillets were cooked. Cook over medium heat until leeks are tender but not brown. Carefully add sherry to pan and STAND BACK as it may flame. Add lobster stock and cook until liquid is reduced by half. Add cream and cook until liquid is reduced by one-third. Season with salt and white pepper to taste. Toss in lobster at last minute so it doesn't get tough.

Place a grouper in each of four shallow bowls. Spoon sauce over fillet and sprinkle with parsley.

SERVES 4

Lacquered Sea Bass in Cioppino Broth

Richard Walter, Executive Chef
Aleathea's at The Inn of Cape May

1½ cups light soy sauce

3 cups mirin

1 tablespoon brown sugar

1 stalk lemon grass, chopped

1 tablespoon plus 2 tablespoons chopped garlic

1 tablespoon chopped ginger

4 (8-ounce) portions Chilean sea bass fillets

2 tablespoons olive oil

¾ bag fresh spinach

Kosher salt and black pepper to taste

Cioppino Broth (Recipe appears on page 103.)

8 snow pea shoots

Combine soy sauce, mirin, brown sugar, lemon grass, 1 tablespoon garlic, and ginger in a saucepan. Bring to a boil, then reduce heat and simmer for approximately 5 to 10 minutes so that flavors steep.

Remove all but 1 cup marinade from pan and cool. Marinate sea bass in cooled marinade for 2 hours.

Heat remaining 1 cup marinade over medium heat. Cook until sauce reduces by half and reaches a "lacquer" consistency. Reserve.

Heat 1 tablespoon olive oil in a sauté pan over medium heat. Add 2 tablespoons garlic and spinach and sauté for about 5 minutes. Season with salt and pepper. Reserve.

Preheat oven to 350°. Heat remaining oil in sauté pan. Sear fillets on all sides. Transfer to oven and cook until desired doneness, about 8 to 10 minutes.

Ladle cioppino broth into four bowls. Place spinach in centers of bowls. Cover with sea bass. Brush sea bass with lacquer. Garnish with snow pea shoots.

SERVES 4

Chilean Sea Bass Papillotte with Tomato Reduction

Christian Rife, Head Chef
Axelsson's Blue Claw Restaurant

4 (6 ounces) boneless, skinless Chilean sea bass fillets
3 ounces clarified butter
Tomato Reduction (Recipe appears on page 132.)
Salt and pepper
Hollandaise sauce, optional

Preheat oven to 375°. Cut 4 pieces parchment paper into large circles, approximately 12 inches round.

Brush parchment paper rounds with clarified butter. Place approximately ½ cup tomato reduction in the center of each circle. Place fillets over reduction. Season with salt and pepper.

Fold parchment so all edges are tightly sealed. Brush tops of paper packages with clarified butter and place on a baking sheet. Bake for 12 to 18 minutes, depending on thickness of fish.

Remove fish from oven. Slice open parchment and top fish with remaining tomato reduction. Optionally, create a tomato fondue reduction by combining remaining reduction with prepared hollandaise sauce.

SERVES 4

Axelsson's Blue Claw Restaurant

Web site: www.blueclawrestaurant.com

Cuisine: prime seafood

Open: all year **Serves:** dinner, drinks

Known for: European ambiance, cherry wood pub,
George Caravan on the baby grand

Most requested table: in the clipper ship area

Years in Business: 22

Flounder Francaise
with Sweet Lemon Sauce

Jay Bush, Chef
Elaine's Dinner Theater

2 cups chicken stock
½ cup lemon juice
½ cup sugar
2 eggs
6 ounces Parmesan cheese
Pinch of dried parsley
8 ounces milk
4 (6 ounces) flounder fillets
Butter to taste
12 (16/20 count) shrimp, cleaned and deveined
Lemon juice to taste
White wine to taste

Combine chicken stock, lemon juice, and sugar in a saucepan. Bring to a boil and simmer until reduced by half. Reserve.

Preheat oven to 350°. Combine eggs, Parmesan cheese, parsley, and milk. Dip fillets into egg batter. Spray a nonstick skillet with cooking spray and warm over medium heat. Place fillets in pan and cook on both sides until fillets are golden brown. Transfer fillets to an ovenproof pan and bake for 5 to 6 minutes.

Meanwhile, heat a small amount of butter in skillet. Add shrimp, lemon juice, and white wine. Sauté until shrimp are cooked through. Top fillets with shrimp and cover with sauce.

SERVES 4

Pelican Club Crab Cakes

Walter J. Jurusz, Executive Chef
The Pelican Club

1 pound jumbo lump crabmeat
1 clove garlic, diced
¼ cup diced Spanish onion
1 green bell pepper, diced
2 egg yolks
⅔ cup mayonnaise
5 slices white bread, crusts removed, cubed
1 teaspoon hot sauce
2 tablespoons lemon juice
1 tablespoon chopped parsley
1 tablespoon chopped chives
Kosher salt to taste
Fresh ground pepper to taste
4 ounces Japanese breadcrumbs
Roasted Yellow Pepper Aïoli (Recipe appears on page 80.)

Clean shells from crabmeat. Reserve in refrigerator.

Sauté garlic, onion, and green pepper until onion is translucent. Remove from heat and cool.

Mix egg yolks and mayonnaise together. Add cubed bread and stir into mixture. Add hot sauce, lemon juice, parsley, chives, salt, and black pepper. Add garlic mixture. Gently fold in crabmeat. Chill well.

Form into 6 cakes. Coat with Japanese breadcrumbs.

Preheat oven to 350°. Heat a sauté pan over medium-high heat. Sauté cakes on one side until lightly brown. Flip onto a cookie tray and bake until golden brown on both sides, about 3 to 8 minutes. Top with roasted yellow pepper aïoli.

SERVES 6

Farfalle with Smoked Salmon and Asparagus

Harry Gleason, Chef/Owner
Daniel's on Broadway

8 ounces farfalle pasta
2 tablespoons butter
1 large shallot, finely chopped
½ cup white wine
2 cups heavy cream
½ cup grated Parmesan cheese
¼ cup horseradish
2 tablespoons coarsely chopped fresh dill
Salt and pepper to taste
2 cups 1-inch pieces asparagus, blanched
6 ounces smoked salmon, cut into 1-inch pieces
½ cup finely chopped tomatoes, optional

Cook farfalle according to package directions until al dente. Drain.

Meanwhile, melt butter in a large sauté pan. Add shallot and sauté until soft. Add white wine and cook until liquid is reduced by half. Add heavy cream to wine and cook until liquid is reduced by one-quarter. Whisk in Parmesan cheese. Add horseradish and dill. Season to taste with salt and pepper.

Add asparagus. Slowly add hot pasta, mixing until coated. Gently fold in salmon. Transfer to serving dishes. Garnish with chopped tomatoes, if you like.

SERVES 4 TO 6

Lobster Pasta

Alyn Toth, Chef
The Mad Batter Restaurant

4 (4 to 6 ounces) lobster tails
1 to 2 cloves garlic, chopped
2 shallots, chopped
½ cup sliced mushrooms
½ cup white wine
1 (12 to 16 ounces) can tomatoes with juice
1½ cups heavy cream
¼ cup lobster stock, optional
Salt and pepper to taste
8 ounces cooked pasta

Remove lobster meat from tails. Cut meat into chunks. Reserve.

Sauté garlic, shallots, and mushrooms in a hot pan until shallots are translucent. Add lobster and sauté for 1 minute. Add wine and deglaze pan. Cook until liquid is reduced by half. Add tomatoes and simmer for 1 minute. Add heavy cream and stock, if desired, and simmer until liquid is reduced by half or has reached a slightly thick consistency. Season with salt and pepper. Toss with pasta and serve.

SERVES 4 TO 6

The Mad Batter Restaurant

Web site: www.madbatter.com

Cuisine: seafood

Open: all year **Serves:** lunch, dinner, brunch, and drinks

Known for: breakfast and lunch

Most requested table: front porch (in season)

Years in Business: 27

Veggie Burgers

David Biondi, Chef
Zoe's Restaurant

1 head broccoli, thick stem removed
1 head cauliflower, thick stem removed
1 zucchini, peeled
2 small carrots, peeled
1 bag raw spinach
4 eggs
3 cups flour
5 shakes garlic juice
Olive oil
10 Kaiser rolls
Lettuce leaves, optional
Tomato slices, optional

Chop all veggies, except spinach, into generous chunks. Place in a large pot. Cover with spinach. Fill pot with 6 to 8 inches of water. Cook on high for approximately 15 minutes until veggies are steamed. Drain well, being sure to get all the water out. Let cool.

When cooled, add eggs, flour, and garlic juice and mix well.

Heat a large skillet or griddle over medium-high heat. Coat with olive oil. Using an ice cream scoop, measure out mixture and place on skillet. Flatten a little to form patties. Sauté until cooked through on both sides. Serve on roll with lettuce and tomato, if you like.

YIELDS 10 BURGERS

Grilled Veggie Hoagies

David Biondi, Chef
Zoe's Restaurant

1 cup chopped green bell pepper
1 cup chopped onion
1 cup chopped zucchini
1 cup chopped mushrooms
12 slices red tomato
½ cup marinara sauce (Your favorite brand is best.)
6 slices white American cheese
2 9 to 9½-inch hoagie rolls

Preheat grill. Lay all vegetables flat on grill. Cover with lid and let vegetables steam for about 3 minutes or until tender.

Remove from grill and place in a bowl. Stir in marinara sauce. Divide mixture between rolls. Cover vegetables with cheese and place under preheated broiler until melted. (Enjoy, but remember ... the filling will be very hot.)

SERVES 2

Zoe's Restaurant

Open: seasonally
Serves: breakfast, lunch, and dinner
Most requested table: outside on the patio
Menu: family casual, cafe
Known for: fresh roasted turkey and roast beef, great muffins
Years in business: 9

Side Dishes
& Sauces

Brandy Carrots
Vegetable Confetti
Coconut-Chipotle Risotto
Chalfonte Eggplant Casserole
Potato Casserole
Potato-Spinach Pancakes
Tomato Reduction
Helen's Thick Cream Sauce

Brandy Carrots

Ed Henry, Owner
Henry's on the Beach

1 cup brandy
½ cup sugar
1 pound unsalted butter
3 pounds carrots, peeled and julienned

Heat brandy over low heat. Add sugar and cook until dissolved. Add butter and melt. Simmer for 10 minutes.

   Meanwhile, steam carrots until cooked. Drain. Add to brandy mixture and serve.

SERVES 8

Vegetable Confetti

Harry Gleason, Chef/Owner
Daniel's on Broadway

1 pound carrots, peeled and julienned
2 ribs celery, julienned
1 red bell pepper, julieneed
1 green bell pepper, julienned
½ red onion, julienned
¼ cup chopped scallions
2 tablespoons chopped garlic
2 tablespoons chopped pickled ginger
1 tablespoon sesame seeds
¼ cup sesame oil
¼ cup light soy sauce

Place all ingredients in a bowl. Toss well. Refrigerate until ready to serve.

SERVES 4

Daniel's on Broadway

Chef: Harry Gleason

Chef's Training: self taught by his mother and grandmother

Favorite Foods: turkey hoagie with provolone (dry, no lettuce)

Coconut-Chipotle Risotto

Neil R. Elsohn, Executive Chef/Owner
Waters Edge Restaurant

2 tablespoons butter
1 onion, finely minced
1½ cups Arborio rice
1 teaspoon salt
½ cup dry white wine or leftover champagne
6 cups chicken stock
¼ cup Coco Lopez
1 tablespoon pureed chipotle pepper in adobo sauce
1 egg, lightly beaten
Kosher salt to taste

Heat butter in a skillet over medium heat. Add onion and cook until translucent but not brown.

Add rice and stir well to coat with butter and onions. Add salt and wine. Stir constantly until wine is absorbed. Add chicken stock, 1 cup at a time, adding more stock as rice absorbs previous stock. Halfway through the stock process, add Coco Lopez and chipotle puree.

Continue to cook, stirring and adding stock, until rice is almost done, about 25 minutes.

Remove from heat. Stir in egg. Adjust seasoning to taste.

SERVES 4

Chalfonte Eggplant Casserole

Dot Burton and Lucille Thompson, Chefs
The Chalfonte Hotel

5 medium eggplants, diced

6 medium onions, diced

4 (28 ounces) cans peeled tomatoes, well drained

¼ cup Worcestershire sauce

2 teaspoons salt

1 teaspoon pepper

1 cup Helen's Thick Cream Sauce (Recipe appears on page 132.)

¼ cup melted bacon grease or vegetable oil

3 tablespoons margarine or butter

2 tablespoons breadcrumbs

1½ cups freshly grated sharp cheese

Paprika to taste

Simmer eggplants and onions in a large pot until tender. Drain well. Add tomatoes, Worcestershire sauce, salt, and pepper. Mix in cream sauce. Stir in bacon grease and 2 tablespoons margarine.

Preheat oven to 450°. Melt remaining 1 tablespoon margarine in a 3-quart casserole dish. Sprinkle 1 tablespoon breadcrumbs over margarine. Add eggplant mixture. Sprinkle remaining crumbs, cheese, and paprika over eggplant mixture. Brown in oven until heated through.

SERVES 12

The Chalfonte Hotel

Chefs: Dot Burton and Lucille Thompson

Chefs' Training: 50 years of cooking at The Chalfonte

Hobbies: family, church activities

Favorite Foods: what they cook!

Potato Casserole

**Nan Hawkins, Innkeeper
Barnard Good House**

4 cups peeled and shredded potatoes
¼ cup water
½ cup milk
3 tablespoons butter
2 eggs
1½ teaspoons salt
Pepper to taste
1 medium onion, diced
Paprika to taste

Preheat oven to 375°. Butter a medium casserole dish.

Place shredded potatoes in water to keep from discoloring. Set aside. Place ¼ cup water, milk, and butter in a saucepan. Cook over medium heat until just under boiling. Set aside.

Beat together eggs, salt, and pepper. Slowly add milk mixture to eggs, beating continuously. Mix well.

Drain potatoes well in a colander. Combine potatoes, onion, and egg mixture. Spoon mixture into prepared dish. Sprinkle with paprika. Bake uncovered for 50 minutes until edges are crusty.

SERVES 6

Barnard Good House

Web site: www.bedandbreakfast.com/bbc/p219003.asp

Open: seasonally

Serves: breakfast

Known for: rated #1 B&B breakfast in NJ

Most requested room: Box

Years in Business: 22

Potato-Spinach Pancakes

Diane K. Muentz, Chef
Alexander's Inn

1 cup all-purpose flour, sifted
1 teaspoon baking powder
1 teaspoon salt
1 teaspoon sugar
1 cup cooked mashed potatoes
6 ounces or 1½ cups chopped spinach
1 egg, lightly beaten
¼ cup melted butter
¾ cup milk

Combine all ingredients, except milk. Blend in milk slowly until a very thick batter forms. Pour ¼ cup batter onto a heated, lightly greased griddle. Brown on one side. Flip with spatula and brown on other side.

Serve warm as a side with roast pork or poultry. Or for brunch, top pancakes with poached egg and hollandaise sauce.

SERVES 6

Alexander's Inn

Web site: www.alexandersinn.com

Cuisine: continental

Open: all year **Serves:** brunch, dinner

Known for: South Jersey's most beautiful dining room

Most requested table: solarium

Years in Business: 30

Tomato Reduction

Christian Rife, Head Chef
Axelsson's Blue Claw Restaurant

3 cups seeded, diced tomatoes
3 tablespoons chopped scallions
2 tablespoons butter
1 tablespoon chopped garlic
2 teaspoons tarragon
2 teaspoons chopped parsley
2 teaspoons sugar
4 ounces white wine
Salt and pepper

Combine all ingredients in a sauté pan and bring to a boil. Simmer for 5 minutes. Remove from heat. Season to taste with salt and pepper. Use as a side dish or a sauce or topping for chicken, vegetables, and fish, such as Chilean Sea Bass Pappillote (Recipe appears on page 117.).

SERVE 4

Helen's Thick Cream Sauce

Dot Burton and Lucille Thompson, Chefs
The Chalfonte Hotel

3 tablespoons butter
1 cup flour
1 cup milk or light cream, heated
Salt and fresh ground pepper

Melt butter in a heavy-bottomed saucepan. Blend in flour and cook, stirring constantly, for 2 minutes or until paste bubbles a bit. Add hot milk. Bring to a boil, stirring as sauce thickens. Add salt and pepper to taste.

Lower heat and continue stirring for 2 to 3 more minutes until sauce is very thick. Remove from heat. (To cool this sauce for later use, cover with wax paper or pour a film of milk over it to prevent skin from forming.)

YIELDS 1 CUP

San Marzano Tomato Sauce

Walter J. Jurusz, Executive Chef
The Pelican Club

¼ cup pure olive oil
¼ cup minced Spanish onions
1 tablespoon minced garlic
1 (28 ounces) can whole San Marzano tomatoes
½ cup water
1 tablespoon tomato paste
10 to 15 basil leaves, chopped
1 teaspoon chopped thyme
1 teaspoon kosher salt
½ teaspoon fresh cracked black pepper

Heat oil in a saucepan over medium heat. Add onion and garlic and sauté until onion is transparent. Add tomatoes, water, and tomato paste. Crush tomatoes with the back of a spoon. Simmer for 30 to 40 minutes. Add fresh herbs, salt, and pepper. Simmer for 5 minutes more.

The Pelican Club

Web site: www.pelicanclubcapemay.com

Cuisine: New American

Open: all year   **Serves:** breakfast, lunch, dinner, drinks

Known for: amazing ocean views and South Beach ambiance

Most requested table: #19

Years in Business: 2

Desserts

Raspberry Tart

Oma's Hazelnut Torte

Decadent Kahlua

Chocolate Cake

Laisy Daisy Cake

Butterscotch Cake

Apple Spice Cake

Amazin' Raisin Apple Cake

Skillet Upside-down Cake

Normandy Bread Pudding

Applesauce Bread Pudding

Steamed Sticky Toffee Pudding with Vanilla Ice Cream

Honey Crunch Baked Apples

Nice Lemon Dessert

Cape May Mocha

Raspberry Tart

Lucille and Dennis Doherty, Innkeepers
The Dormer House

1½ cups butter
1 cup sugar
1 egg
4 cups all-purpose flour
1 teaspoon salt
1 cup raspberry preserves
½ cup slivered almonds

Preheat oven to 350°.

Cream together butter and sugar. Add egg, flour, and salt. Mix to form a dough. Press two-thirds of dough into the bottom of a 9- or 10-inch tart pan. Cover with preserves.

Roll out remaining dough. Cut into 10 to 14 strips. Place 5 to 7 strips across preserves. Weave a cross-strip through center by first folding back every other strip going the other way. Continue weaving lattice, folding back alternate strips each time a cross-strip is added. Sprinkle with almonds. Bake 35 to 40 minutes.

SERVES 12

The Dormer House

Innkeeper: Lucille and Dennis Doherty
Favorite Foods: Russian Coffee Cake and chocolate
Favorite Cape May Activity: horse and carriage rides

Oma's Hazelnut Torte

Anita and Karsten Dierk, Innkeepers
The Manse Bed and Breakfast Inn

1 pound hazelnuts
12 extra large eggs, separated
1 pound plus 1 cup confectioners' sugar
Pinch of salt
2 teaspoons vanilla extract
1 quart heavy cream

Grind hazelnuts in a food processor. Very important: when grinding the nuts, do not grind to a powder; grind them finer than a rough chop. Reserve.

Preheat oven to 300°. Spray 2 large springform pans with canola oil.

Beat egg whites until stiff. Set aside. In a separate bowl, beat yolks and 1 pound confectioners' sugar until foamy and creamy. Add salt during beating process. Add nuts and 1 teaspoon vanilla to yolk mixture. (Batter will become stiff.) Fold egg whites into mixture. Pour batter into prepared pans.

Bake for approximately 45 minutes or until tester comes out clean. When cooled, remove from pans. Slice cakes horizontally so each cake is in two sections.

Whip heavy cream with remaining 1 cup confectioners' sugar and 1 teaspoon vanilla. Spread cream mixture between cake halves.

You will have a cake to keep and one to give away! Or, if you prefer, you can make a four-layer cake with the cream mixture between each layer. Be sure to anchor the layers with bakers sticks so they don't slide. Enjoy!

SERVES 8

The Manse Bed and Breakfast Inn

Innkeepers: Anita and Karsten Dierk

Favorite Foods: Anita - Anita's Burritas and Corn-Tomato Salsa;
Karsten - Oma's Hazelnut Torte

Favorite Cape May Activity: Anita - attending theater and music
festivals, boat trips around Cape May, dining at The Washington Inn
Karsten - fishing

Decadent Kahlua Chocolate Cake

Lorraine and Terry Schmidt, Owners/Innkeepers
The Humphrey Hughes House

1 cup strong coffee
½ cup plus 2 tablespoons Kahlua
5 ounces unsweetened baking chocolate
1 cup plus 1 tablespoon butter
2 cups sugar
2 cups all-purpose flour
1 teaspoon baking soda
¼ teaspoon salt
2 eggs
1 teaspoon vanilla extract
4 ounces semi-sweet chocolate

Preheat oven to 275°. Grease a Bundt pan and dust with sifted cocoa.

Heat coffee and ½ cup Kahlua in a double boiler over simmering water. Add chocolate and 1 cup butter and stir frequently until melted. When mixture is smooth, add sugar and stir until dissolved. Remove from heat and cool until lukewarm. Reserve.

In a mixing bowl, sift together flour, baking soda, and salt. Gradually add coffee mixture, beating well after each addition to avoid lumps. Add eggs and vanilla. Beat with an electric mixer at medium speed for 2 minutes.

Pour batter into prepared pan. Bake for 1½ hours or until a toothpick inserted in center comes out clean. Cool.

Melt remaining 1 tablespoon butter and semi-sweet chocolate in a double boiler over simmering water. Add remaining 2 tablespoons Kahlua, adding more if necessary to achieve a "spreadable" consistency. Spread glaze over cake.

SERVES 14

Laisy Daisy Cake

Elizabeth and Niels Favre, Innkeepers
Canterbury Cottage Inn B&B

1 cup sugar
2 eggs
1 cup flour
1 teaspoon baking powder
Pinch of salt
2 tablespoons butter
½ cup milk, hot
½ cup butter, melted
½ cup coconut
⅔ cup brown sugar, packed
4 tablespoons heavy cream

Preheat oven to 350°.

Mix together sugar and eggs. In a separate bowl, sift together dry ingredients and add to sugar and eggs. Soften 2 tablespoons butter in hot milk and add to batter. Pour into an 8 x 8-inch pan. Bake for 15 to 20 minutes or until cake begins to brown.

Meanwhile, combine the 4 remaining ingredients. When cake has finished baking, spread topping on hot cake. Set oven to broil. Put cake under broiler for 3 to 4 minutes or until topping turns brown. Cool on a wire rack. Cut into squares.

YIELDS 12 PIECES

Butterscotch Cake

Barbara Masemore, Innkeeper
Inn at 22 Jackson

1 (3.4 ounces) box butterscotch pudding (not instant)
2 cups milk
1 box yellow cake mix
1 (12 ounces) bag butterscotch morsels
1 cup chopped nuts

Preheat oven to 350°. Grease a 9 x 13-inch baking pan.

Combine pudding mix and milk in a large glass bowl. Microwave on high for 3 minutes. Stir. Cook for 3 minutes more or until thick. Stir in cake mix. Pour into prepared pan. Sprinkle with butterscotch morsels and nuts. Bake for 30 minutes.

SERVES 12 TO 15

Inn at 22 Jackson

Web site: www.innat22jackson.com

Open: all year

Serves: breakfast and afternoon tea

Known for: gorgeous home, great food, whimsical atmosphere

Most requested room: Each is terrific!

Years in Business: 10

Apple Spice Cake

Carrie O'Sullivan, Innkeeper
Victorian Lace Inn

6 apples, peeled and sliced
2 cups sugar
1 cup canola oil
2 eggs
3 cups sifted flour
2 teaspoons baking soda
½ teaspoon salt
2 teaspoons cinnamon
1 teaspoon nutmeg
1 cup chopped walnuts
Sugar

Preheat oven to 350°. Grease a 9 x 13-inch pan.

Place apple slices into a bowl and cover with sugar. Let stand for 5 to 10 minutes. Combine oil and eggs and pour over apples.

In a separate bowl, mix remaining ingredients and add to apple mixture. Stir well. Pour into prepared pan. Bake for 50 minutes.

Cool and sprinkle with granulated sugar before serving.

SERVES 12 TO 15

Victorian Lace Inn

Web site: www.victorianlaceinn.com

Open: all year

Serves: brunch and afternoon tea

Known for: warm hospitality and tastefully appointed suites

Most requested room: Bantry Cottage

Amazin' Raisin Apple Cake

Toby and Andy Fontaine, Innkeepers
Bayberry Inn

2 cups sugar

1 cup mayonnaise

⅓ cup milk

2 eggs

3 cups flour

2 teaspoons baking soda

2 teaspoons ground cinnamon

½ teaspoon ground nutmeg

½ teaspoon salt

¼ teaspoon ground cloves

3 cups peeled and chopped Granny Smith apples

1 cup raisins, soaked in warm water

½ cup chopped pecans

Preheat oven to 350°. Coat a tube pan with nonstick spray.

Mix together sugar, mayonnaise, milk, and eggs in a large bowl. In a separate bowl, combine dry ingredients. Add dry ingredients to wet and mix for 2 minutes. Stir in apples, raisins, and pecans. Pour batter into prepared pan. Bake for approximately 45 minutes.

SERVES 12 TO 16

Bayberry Inn

Web site: www.bayberryinncapemay.com

Open: all year

Serves: breakfast and afternoon tea

Known for: generous 3-course breakfasts

Most requested room: Sunshine Room

Years in Business: 2

Skillet Upside-down Cake

Lenanne and James Labrusciano, Owners/Innkeepers
The Albert Stevens Inn

1 cup flour
1 teaspoon double-acting baking powder
4 egg yolks
1 tablespoon butter, melted
1 teaspoon vanilla
4 egg whites
1 cup sugar
½ cup butter
1 cup brown sugar, packed
1 (8 ounces) can pineapple rings
Maraschino cherries

Preheat oven to 350°.

Sift together flour and baking powder. In a separate bowl, beat egg yolks. Stir in melted butter and vanilla. Add flour mixture and stir to combine.

In a third bowl, beat egg whites until stiff. Add sugar, 1 tablespoon at a time. Combine egg white mixture with flour mixture. Reserve batter.

Melt ½ cup butter in a 9- or 10-inch ovenproof heavy skillet over medium heat. Add brown sugar and stir until sugar dissolves. Remove from heat. Place pineapple rings in skillet. Place a cherry in the middle of each ring. Cover with batter and place in oven. Bake for 30 minutes. When cooled, turn cake out of skillet and onto a plate.

SERVES 6 TO 8

The Albert Stevens Inn

Innkeepers: Lenanne and James Labrusciano

Favorite Cape May Activity: dining at the numerous,
wonderful restaurants in Cape May

Normandy Bread Pudding

Toby and Andy Fontaine, Innkeepers
Bayberry Inn

2 cups milk
4 tablespoons butter
2 eggs
½ cup sugar
1 teaspoon cinnamon
Pinch of salt
2½ to 3 cups broken bits of firm bread

Preheat oven to 350°.

Heat milk and butter in a pan until butter is melted and milk is just hot. Meanwhile, whisk together eggs, sugar, cinnamon, and salt.

Place bread in a 2-quart casserole dish. Combine egg and milk mixtures and pour over bread. Set casserole dish in a pan of hot water so that water comes up the side about 1½ inches. Bake for 40 minutes.

SERVES 4

Applesauce Bread Pudding

Dane and Joan Wells, Innkeepers
The Queen Victoria® Bed and Breakfast

16 slices cinnamon or raisin bread
½ cup butter, softened
2 cups applesauce
1 cup brown sugar, packed
4 teaspoons cinnamon
½ teaspoon nutmeg
1 cup raisins, optional
4 cups milk
4 eggs
2 teaspoons vanilla
Whipped or light cream, optional

Preheat oven to 350°. Spray a 3-quart glass baking dish with nonstick spray.

Spread both sides of each bread slice with butter. Fit half the bread snugly into bottom of prepared dish, cutting bread to fit as necessary. Spread applesauce on top. Mix sugar and spices and sprinkle on top of applesauce. Cover with raisins, if desired, and remaining buttered bread.

In a separate bowl, blend milk, eggs, and vanilla. Pour over ingredients in baking dish. (This dish may be prepared in advance to this point. Cover and refrigerate for up to 24 hours.) Bake for 45 to 60 minutes until lightly puffed and browned. Serve with whipped or light cream, if desired.

SERVES 12

Steamed Sticky Toffee Pudding with Vanilla Ice Cream

Andrew J. Carthy, Chef
The Ebbitt Room at The Virginia Hotel

½ cup pitted and chopped dates
½ cup water
¼ cup butter, softened
½ cup dark brown sugar, packed
1 egg
¾ cup sifted flour
1 teaspoon baking powder
½ teaspoon baking soda
Toffee Sauce (see recipe)
Fresh berries, optional
Mint leaves, optional

Butter four 4-ounce ramekin or custard cups.

Combine dates and water in a small pot and bring to a boil. Cook for 1 minute and remove from heat. Cool for approximately 10 minutes. Puree and set aside.

Beat butter and sugar in a mixer or with an electric beater on high until light and fluffy. Add egg and mix until smooth. Lower speed and add flour and baking powder. Stir baking soda into date mixture. Fold into batter.

Scoop mixture into prepared cups. Steam for 30 minutes or until set. Remove from steamer and cool slightly before unmolding.

Place each toffee pudding in center of dessert plate. Cover with toffee sauce. Place a scoop of vanilla ice cream on top. Garnish with fresh berries and mint, if you like.

SERVES 4

Toffee Sauce

Andrew J. Carthy, Chef
The Ebbitt Room at The Virginia Hotel

1 pound sugar
⅓ cup water
½ teaspoon lemon juice
2 tablespoons light corn syrup
1½ cups heavy cream
½ cup butter

Place sugar, water, and lemon juice in a heavy-bottomed saucepan over medium-high heat. Bring to a boil, brushing down the sides of pot with a brush dipped in water.

Add corn syrup and cook until golden amber in color. Remove from heat and carefully stir in cream. Add butter a little at a time. Serve over Sticky Toffee Pudding, ice cream, or your favorite dessert.

The Ebbitt Room at The Virginia Hotel

Chef: Andrew J. Carthy

Chef's Training: self-taught

Hobbies: travel, soccer, reading

Favorite Foods: Indian and Italian

Honey Crunch Baked Apples

Joe and JoAnne Tornambe, Innkeepers
Woodleigh House B&B

6 large apples (I prefer Rome or Winesap.)
⅓ cup granola (I make my own granola, but you can buy ready-made.)
½ teaspoon cinnamon
¼ teaspoon nutmeg
2 teaspoons lemon juice
6 tablespoons honey
3 tablespoons butter, melted
¾ cup apple juice

Preheat oven to 350°.

Core apples. Stand upright in a baking dish. Combine granola, cinnamon, nutmeg, lemon juice, and 3 tablespoons honey. Spoon equal amounts of mixture into center of each apple. Combine remaining honey with butter and apple juice. Pour over apples. Bake 45 minutes, basting several times with pan liquids. Enjoy!

SERVES 6

Nice Lemon Dessert

Toby and Andy Fontaine, Innkeepers
Bayberry Inn

1 cup sugar
4 tablespoons flour
¼ teaspoon salt
Grated rind of ½ lemon
3 tablespoons lemon juice
2 eggs, separated
1 cup milk
1 tablespoon butter, softened

Preheat oven to 325°.

Combine sugar, flour, and salt. Add lemon rind and juice.

In a separate bowl, beat egg yolks, milk, and butter. Add to lemon mixture. In a third bowl, beat egg whites until stiff and fold into batter.

Pour batter into an ovenproof bowl. Set bowl in a pan of hot water so water comes up the side about 1½ inches.

Bake for approximately 50 minutes. (You'll know it's done, when you insert a knife around the sides and no liquid is left.)

SERVES 2 TO 4

Cape May Mocha

Mrs. Marie Wedemeyer and Dr. Ellen ME Wedemeyer, Owners
Wedemeyer's Cape May Coffee, Tea, and Gifts

¼ ounce peach syrup
¼ ounce amaretto syrup
2 ounces brewed espresso
1 ounce Ghirardelli white chocolate syrup
8 ounces steamed milk

Combine peach and amaretto syrups and espresso in a clear 12-ounce mug. Stir until well combined. Drizzle Ghirardelli white chocolate syrup down the sides of mug.

Pour steamed milk into mug. Stir to combine with syrups and espresso. Top with froth from steamed milk. Garnish with Ghirardelli white chocolate drizzle.

SERVES 1

Wedemeyer's Cape May Coffee, Tea, and Gifts

Web site: www.capemay.com/coffee

Cuisine: gourmet breakfast sandwiches, wraps, desserts, espresso drinks

Open: all year **Serves:** breakfast, lunch, brunch, drinks

Known for: atmosphere—Cape May's finest gourmet coffee house

Most requested table: by the window facing Peaches

Years in Business: 10

Index

A

A Ca Mia 78, 81
Abigail Adams Bed & Breakfast By The
   Sea 29, 36, 71
Aïoli, Roasted Yellow Pepper 80
Aleathea's at The Inn of Cape May
   103, 116
Alexander's Inn 131
Almond
   Black Raspberry Almond Bars 62
   Coffee Toffee Bars 63
   Macaroons 58
   No Bake Chocolate-Topped Nut Chews
      69
   Raspberry Tart 136
Amazin' Raisin Apple Cake 142
Angel of the Sea Bed & Breakfast
   60, 61, 65
Apples
   Amazin' Raisin Apple Cake 142
   Apple Spice Cake 141
   Applesauce Bread Pudding 145
   German Apple Pancakes 36
   Honey Crunch Baked Apples 148
   Oven Baked Apple French Toast 28
   Sunrise Casserole 14
   Whole Wheat Apple Pancakes 35
Applesauce Bread Pudding 145
Artichokes
   Spinach and Artichokes in Puff Pastry
      85
Asparagus
   Farfalle with Smoked Salmon 120
Axelsson's Blue Claw Restaurant 117, 132

B

Bacon
   Caramelized Onion, Spinach, and Bacon
      Quiche 20
Baked Swiss Cheese Omelet 16
Bananas
   Bread 75
   Bread French Toast 25
   Chocolate Chip Muffins 43
   Fruit Pizza 37
   Fruits of Summer Souffle 38
   Granola Delight 42

Barnard Good House 46, 100, 130
Bars. *See also* Cookies
   Black Raspberry Almond 62
   Butter Finger 64
   Chocolate Praline 65
   Coffee Toffee 63
   Frosted Peanut Butter Brownies 67
   Mom's Brownies 66
   Strawberry 61
Basil
   Bruschetta Tomatoes 81
   Marinated Tomatoes 91
   Mussels in Tomato-Basil Gorgonzola
      Broth 93
   Tapenade 79
Bayberry Inn 83, 142, 144, 149
Bean, Black Sauce 95
Beauclaire's Bed & Breakfast 26
Bedford Inn 31, 34, 62
Beef
   Cape Fillet 110
   Roasted Fillet of Beef with Blue Cheese-
      Horseradish Cream 111
Bell peppers
   Grilled Veggie Hoagies 123
   Herb Chicken 106
   Roasted Stuffed Pepper 90
   Roasted Yellow Pepper Aïoli 80
   Vegetable Confetti 127
Blue Cheese-Horseradish Cream 111
Blueberries.
   Blueberry Compote 49
   Coffee Cake 73
   French Toast Strata 27
   Fruit Pizza 37
   Fruits of Summer Souffle 38
Brandy Carrots 126
Bread
   Applesauce Bread Pudding 145
   Banana 75
   Banana Bread French Toast 25
   Banana Chocolate Chip Muffins 43
   Bannoch 46
   Egg Baskets 13
   Habit Forming Cinnamon Buns 47
   Ham and Cheese Croissants 23
   Honey Baked French Toast 29
   Normandy Bread Pudding 144

Orange Cranberry Bread 74
Orange Toast 26
Orange Walnut Muffins 45
Oven Baked Apple French Toast 28
Peach French Toast 24
Sunrise Casserole 14
Swiss Custard 15
Walnut-encrusted French Toast 30
Broccoli
    Ham and Broccoli Frittata 17
    Smoked Turkey and Cheese Quiche 18
    Veggie Burgers 122
Brownies. *See* Bars
    Frosted Peanut Butter 67
    Mom's 66
Bruschetta Tomatoes 81
Butter
    Scones 54
    Strawberry 48
Butter Finger Bars 64
Butterscotch Cake 140

C

Cakes
    Amazin' Raisin Apple Cake 142
    Apple Spice Cake 141
    Butterscotch Cake 140
    Decadent Kahlua Chocolate Cake 138
    Laisy Daisy Cake 139
    Oma's Hazelnut Torte 137
    Skillet Upside-down Cake 143
Candies
    Butter Finger Bars 64
    Chocolate Praline Bars 65
    Decadent Candy 68
    No Bake Chocolate-Topped Nut Chews
        69
Canterbury Cottage Inn B&B
        25, 75, 139
Cape Fillet of Beef 110
Cape May Mocha 150
Captain Mey's Bed & Breakfast Inn
        35, 56
Caramelized Onion, Spinach, and Bacon
        Quiche 20
Carrots
    Brandy 126
    Vegetable Confetti 127
    Veggie Burgers 122
Casserole
    Chalfonte Eggplant 129

French Toast Strata 27
Potato 130
Sunrise Casserole 14
Swiss Custard 15
Cereal
    Baked Peaches with Crunch Topping 41
    Butter Finger Bars 64
    Fruit Pizza 37
    Granola Delight 42
    Honey Crunch Baked Apples 148
Chalfonte Eggplant Casserole 129
Cheese
    -Straw Daisy Crackers 53
    Baked Swiss Cheese Omelet 16
    Blue Cheese-Horseradish Cream 111
    Chalfonte Eggplant Casserole 129
    Chicken Mascarpone 107
    Egg Baskets 13
    Elegant Spinach Pie 83
    Four Cheese Herb Quiche 19
    Granola Delight 42
    Ham and Broccoli Frittata 17
    Ham and Cheese Croissants 23
    Heirloom Tomato Salad 97
    Herb Chicken 106
    Mussels in Tomato-Basil Gorgonzola
        Broth 93
    Poached Peaches with White Cheese
        Mousse 40
    Ricotta Cheese Cookies 60
    Ricotta Pancakes 34
    Roasted Stuffed Pepper 90
    Rum Raisin Cheddar Spread 52
    Savory Crab Dip 78
    Smoked Turkey and Cheese Quiche 18
    Sunrise Casserole 14
    Swiss Custard 15
    Three Sisters Quesadilla 86
Chicken. *See also* Poultry
    Herb Chicken 106
    Mascarpone 107
Chilean Sea Bass. *See* Sea Bass
Chinese Tortellini 84
Chipotle
    Coconut-Chipotle Risotto 128
Chocolate
    Banana Chocolate Chip Muffins 43
    Butter Finger Bars 64
    Coffee Toffee Bars 63
    Cookies 56
    Decadent Candy 68
    Decadent Kahlua Chocolate Cake 138

Frosted Peanut Butter Brownies 67
Mom's Brownies 66
No Bake Chocolate-Topped Nut Chews
  69
Praline Bars 65
Cinnamon Buns 47
Cinnamon Coffee Cake 71
Cioppino Broth 103
Coconut
  -Chipotle Risotto 128
  Laisy Daisy Cake 139
  Macaroons 59
  Orange Vinaigrette 99
Coffee
  Cape May Mocha 150
  Toffee Bars 63
Coffee Cake. *See also* Cakes
  Blueberry 73
  Cinnamon 71
  Russian 72
  Velia's 70
Cold Cranberry Soup 100
Compote, Blueberry 49
Cookies. *See also* Bars
  Almond Macaroons 58
  Chocolate 56
  Hamantaschen 57
  Ricotta Cheese 60
Corn
  Fresh Corn Quiche 22
  Grouper Charleston 115
  Three Sisters Quesadilla 86
  Tomato-Corn Salsa 82
Crab
  Chicken Mascarpone 107
  Savory Crab Dip 78
Cranberry
  Cold Cranberry Soup 100
  Orange Cranberry Bread 74
Cream cheese
  Eggs Mey 11
  French Toast Strata 27
  Fruits of Summer Souffle 38
  Peach Pillows 31
  Rum Raisin Cheddar Spread 52
Cream Scones 55
Crispy Herb Risotto Cake 108
Croissants
  Ham and Cheese 23
  Peach Pillows 31

D

Daniel's on Broadway
  95, 108, 115, 120, 127
Decadent Candy 68
Decadent Kahlua Chocolate Cake 138
Desserts
  Amazin' Raisin Apple Cake 142
  Apple Spice Cake 141
  Applesauce Bread Pudding 145
  Butterscotch Cake 140
  Decadent Kahlua Chocolate Cake 138
  Honey Crunch Baked Apples 148
  Laisy Daisy Cake 139
  Nice Lemon Dessert 149
  Normandy Bread Pudding 144
  Oma's Hazelnut Torte 137
  Raspberry Tart 136
  Skillet Upside-down Cake 143
  Steamed Sticky Toffee Pudding 146
Duck, Pan-Roasted Breast 108

E

Eggplant, Chalfonte Casserole 129
Eggs
  Baked Swiss Cheese Omelet 16
  Baskets 13
  Caramelized Onion, Spinach, and Bacon
    Quiche 20
  Florentine 12
  Four Cheese Herb Quiche 19
  Fresh Corn Quiche 22
  Ham and Broccoli Frittata 17
  Ham and Cheese Croissants 23
  Mey 11
  Poached Eggs on Brioche 10
  Smoked Turkey and Cheese Quiche 18
  Sunrise Casserole 14
  Swiss Custard 15
Elaine's Dinner Theater 118
Elegant Spinach Pie 83
Escargot in Garlic Cream 94
Escarole, Warm Salad 98

F

Fairthorne Bed & Breakfast 27, 38, 49
Farfalle with Smoked Salmon and
    Asparagus 120
Field Green Salad 96
Fish
  Chilean Sea Bass Papillotte 117

Flounder Francaise with Sweet Lemon
    Sauce 118
Grouper Charleston 115
Hazelnut Vanilla Crusted Halibut 114
Lacquered Sea Bass in Cioppino Broth
    116
Peppered Ahi Tuna with Black Bean
    Sauce 95
Tuna with Honey Mustard Ginger Sauce
    113
Flounder Francaise with Sweet Lemon
    Sauce 118
Four Cheese Herb Quiche 19
French Toast
    Banana Bread 25
    Ham and Cheese Croissants 23
    Honey Baked 29
    Orange Toast 26
    Oven Baked Apple 28
    Peach French Toast 24
    Strata 27
    Walnut-encrusted 30
Fresh Corn Quiche 22
Frosted Peanut Butter Brownies 67
Fruit Pizza 37
Fruits of Summer Souffle 38

G

Garlic
    Cioppino Broth 103
    Escargot in Garlic Cream 94
    Mussels in Tomato-Basil Gorgonzola 93
    Roasted Yellow Pepper Aïoli 80
    Warm Escarole Salad 98
Gecko's 86
German Apple Pancakes 36
Ginger
    Pancakes 32
    Vegetable Confetti 127
Gingerbread House 64, 68
Goat cheese
    Field Green Salad 96
    Roasted Stuffed Pepper 90
    Savory Crab Dip 78
Granola
    Delight 42
    Honey Crunch Baked Apples 148
Greens. *See also* Salads
    Field Green Salad 96
    Heirloom Tomato Salad 97
    Roasted Stuffed Pepper 90

Warm Escarole Salad 98
Grilled Veggie Hoagies 123
Grouper Charleston 115

H

Habit Forming Cinnamon Buns 47
Ham
    and Broccoli Frittata 17
    Egg Baskets 13
    Roasted Stuffed Pepper 90
Hamantaschen 57
Hazelnut
    Oma's Hazelnut Torte 137
    Vanilla Crusted Halibut 114
Heirloom Tomato Salad 97
Helen's Thick Cream Sauce 133
Henry's on the Beach 107, 126
Herb Chicken 106
Honey
    Baked French Toast 29
    Crunch Baked Apples 148
    Mustard Ginger Sauce 113
Horseradish Cream 111

I

Ice Cream, Vanilla 146
Inn at 22 Jackson 140
Inn by the Silver Maple 23

L

Lacquered Sea Bass in Cioppino Broth 116
Laisy Daisy Cake 139
Lamb Shank with Dark Rum and Root
    Veggies 112
Leith Hall - Historic Seashore Inn
    54, 58, 66
Lemon
    Nice Lemon Dessert 149
    Sauce 33
    Sweet Lemon Sauce 118
Lobster
    Bisque 102
    Pasta 121
Lucille's Onion Soup 101
Luther Ogden Inn 28

M

Macaroons
    Almond 58
    Coconut 59

Marinated Tomatoes 91
Mom's Brownies 66
Monstrous Sour Cream Muffins 44
Mousse, White Cheese 40
Muffins
    Banana Chocolate Chip 43
    Monstrous Sour Cream 44
Mushrooms
    Cape Fillet of Beef 110
    Cioppino Broth 103
    Elegant Spinach Pie 83
    Escargot in Garlic Cream 94
Mussels
    in Tomato-Basil Gorgonzola Broth 93
    Mekong 92
Mustard, Honey Ginger Sauce 113

N

Nice Lemon Dessert 149
Normandy Bread Pudding 144
Nuts. *See* individual nuts

O

Olives
    Tapenade 79
Oma's Hazelnut Torte 137
Omelet. *See* Eggs
Onions
    Caramelized Onion, Spinach and Bacon
        Quiche 20
    Chalfonte Eggplant Casserole 129
    Elegant Spinach Pie 83
    Grilled Veggie Hoagies 123
    Lucille's Onion Soup 101
    Poached Eggs with Caramelized Onions
        10
Oranges
    Citrus Sections in Vanilla Marinade 39
    Coconut Orange Vinaigrette 99
    Cranberry Bread 74
    Orange Toast 26
    Walnut Muffins 45
Oven Baked Apple French Toast 28

P

Pan-Roasted Duck Breast 108
Pancakes
    German Apple 36
    Ginger 32
    Potato-Spinach 131

Ricotta 34
Whole Wheat Apple 35
Pasta
    Chinese Tortellini 84
    Farfalle with Smoked Salmon and
        Asparagus 120
    Lobster 121
    Mussels in Tomato-Basil Gorgonzola
        Broth 93
Peaches
    Baked Peaches with Crunch Topping 41
    French Toast 24
    Fruits of Summer Souffle 38
    Peach Pillows 31
    Poached with White Cheese Mousse 40
Peaches at Sunset 92, 113
Peanut butter
    Butter Finger Bars 64
    Frosted Peanut Butter Brownies 67
Pecans
    Amazin' Raisin Apple Cake 142
    Banana Bread 75
    Strawberry Bars 61
Pelican Club Crab Cakes 119
Peppered Ahi Tuna with Black Bean Sauce
    95
Peppers. *See* Bell peppers
Pesto
    Chicken Mascarpone 107
Pies
    Elegant Spinach 83
    Raspberry Tart 136
Pineapples
    Skillet Upside-down Cake 143
Poached Eggs on Brioche with Caramelized
    Onions 10
Poached Peaches with White Cheese
    Mousse 40
Potatoes
    -Spinach Pancakes 131
    Casserole 130
Poultry
    Chicken Mascarpone 107
    Herb Chicken 106
    Pan-Roasted Duck Breast 108
Pudding
    Applesauce Bread Pudding 145
    Butterscotch Cake 140
    Normandy Bread Pudding 144
    Steamed Sticky Toffee Pudding 146
Puff Pastry
    Escargot in Garlic Cream 94

Spinach and Artichokes in 85
Pumpkin Seed Vinaigrette 96

Q

Quesadilla, Three Sisters 86
Quiche
    Caramelized Onion, Spinach, and Bacon
      20
    Four Cheese Herb 19
    Fresh Corn 22
    Smoked Turkey and Cheese 18

R

Raisins
    Amazin' Raisin Apple Cake 142
    Applesauce Bread Pudding 145
    Butter Scones 54
    Oven Baked Apple French Toast 28
    Rum Raisin Cheddar Spread 52
Raspberries
    Black Raspberry Almond Bars 62
    Raspberry Tart 136
Rice
    Coconut-Chipotle Risotto 128
    Crispy Herb Risotto Cake 108
Ricotta cheese
    Cookies 60
    Pancakes 34
Risotto
    Coconut-Chipotle 128
    Crispy Risotto Herb Cake 108
Roasted Fillet of Beef with Blue Cheese-
    Horseradish Cream 111
Roasted Yellow Pepper Aïoli 80
Rolled oats
    Baked Peaches with Crunch Topping 41
    Butter Finger Bars 64
    Fruit Pizza 37
Rum
    Lamb Shank with Dark Rum 112
    Raisin Cheddar Spread 52
Russian Coffee Cake 72

S

Salads
    Field Green with Toasted Pumpkin Seed
      Vinaigrette 96
    Heirloom Tomato Salad 97
    Warm Escarole Salad 98
Salmon

Farfalle with Smoked Salmon 120
Salsa, Tomato-Corn 82
Saltwood House Bed & Breakfast
    16, 41, 74
San Marzano Tomato Sauce, 133
Sauce
    Black Bean 95
    Helen's Thick Cream Sauce 132
    Honey Mustard Ginger 113
    Lemon 33
    San Marzano Tomato Sauce 133
    Sweet Lemon 118
    Toffee 147
Sausage
    Sunrise Casserole 14
Savory Crab Dip 78
Scones
    Butter 54
    Cream 55
Sea Bass
    in Cioppino Broth 116
    Papillotte with Tomato Reduction 117
Shrimp
    Chicken Mascarpone 107
    Flounder Francaise 118
Skillet Upside-down Cake 143
Smoked Turkey and Cheese Quiche 18
Soups
    Cioppino Broth 103
    Cold Cranberry 100
    Lobster Bisque 102
    Lucille's Onion Soup 101
Sour cream
    Bannoch Bread 46
    Fruit Pizza 37
    Fruits of Summer Souffle 38
    Ham and Broccoli Frittata 17
    Monstrous Sour Cream Muffins 44
    Ricotta Pancakes 34
    Russian Coffee Cake 72
    Savory Crab Dip 78
Spinach
    and Artichokes in Puff Pastry 85
    Caramelized Onion, Spinach, and Bacon
      Quiche 20
    Eggs Florentine 12
    Elegant Spinach Pie 83
    Potato-Spinach Pancakes 131
    Veggie Burgers 122
Steamed Sticky Toffee Pudding with
    Vanilla Ice Cream 146

Strawberries
  Bars 61
  Butter 48
  Fruit Pizza 37
  Fruits of Summer Souffle 38
Sunrise Casserole 14
Swiss Custard 15

T

Tapenade 79
The Albert Stevens Inn 59, 143
The Chalfonte Hotel 101, 129, 132
The Dormer House 72, 136
The Ebbitt Room at The Virginia Hotel
     97, 146, 147
The Henry Sawyer Inn 45
The Humphrey Hughes House
     48, 55, 138
The Inn at Journey's End 39, 43, 73
The Linda Lee Bed and Breakfast
     17, 19, 67, 85
The Mad Batter Restaurant 121
The Mainstay Inn 22, 37, 53
The Manse Bed and Breakfast Inn
     47, 82, 137
The Pelican Club 80, 93, 119, 133
The Primrose Inn 20
The Puffin 14, 15, 84
The Queen Victoria® Bed and Breakfast
     52, 69, 145
The Sea Villa Hotel 42
The Southern Mansion Bed & Breakfast
     10, 30, 106, 110
The Washington Inn
     79, 90, 91, 99, 102, 111, 114
The Wooden Rabbit 32
Toffee
  Coffee Toffee Bars 63
  Sauce 147
  Steamed Sticky Toffee Pudding 146
Tomatoes
  -Corn Salsa 82
  Bruschetta Tomatoes 81
  Cioppino Broth 103
  Grouper Charleston 115
  Ham and Broccoli Frittata 17
  Heirloom Tomato Salad 97
  Marinated 91
  Mussels in Tomato-Basil Gorgonzola
     Broth 93
  Reduction 117, 132

San Marzano Tomato Sauce, 133
Tuna with Honey Mustard Ginger Sauce
     113
Turkey, Smoked and Cheese Quiche 18

V

Vanilla
  Citrus Sections in Vanilla Marinade 39
  Hazelnut Vanilla Crusted Halibut 114
  Ice Cream 146
Vegetable Confetti 127
Vegetables. *See also* individual vegetables
  Brandy Carrots 126
  Chalfonte Eggplant Casserole 129
  Grilled Veggie Hoagies 123
  Root Veggies 112
  Vegetable Confetti 127
  Veggie Burgers 122
Veggie Burgers 122
Veggie Hoagies 123
Velia's Coffee Cake 70
Velia's Seaside Inn 18, 70
Victorian Lace Inn 24, 141
Vinaigrette
  Coconut Orange 99
  Toasted Pumpkin Seed 96

W

Walnuts
  -encrusted French Toast 30
  Apple Spice Cake 141
  Chocolate Cookies 56
  Fruit Pizza 37
  Orange Walnut Muffins 45
  Velia's Coffee Cake 70
Warm Escarole Salad 98
Waters Edge Restaurant
     94, 96, 98, 112, 128
Wedemeyer's Cape May Coffee, Tea, and
     Gifts 150
Whole Wheat Apple Pancakes 35
Windward House Inn Bed and Breakfast
     12, 40, 63
Woodleigh House B&B 13, 57, 148

Z

Zoe's Restaurant 44, 122, 123
Zucchini
  Grilled Veggie Hoagies 123
  Veggie Burgers 122

books by small potatoes press

Please send the following:

_____ copies of **Cape May Cooks: Recipes from New Jersey's Restaurant Capital** - $9.95

_____ copies of **Philadelphia Flavor: Restaurant Recipes from the City and Suburbs** - $15.95

_____ copies of **Coastal Cuisine: Seaside Recipes from Maine to Maryland** - $11.95

_____ copies of **PB&J USA: Recipes for Kids and Adults by Kids and Adults** - $10.95

Sales Tax: **Cape May Cooks:** NJ addresses please add $.60 (6%) per book
                             Philadelphia Flavor: NJ addresses please add $.96 (6%) per book
                             Coastal Cuisine: NJ addresses please add $.72 (6%) per book
                             PB&J USA: NJ addresses please add $.66 (6%) per book

Shipping: $3.00 for the first book; $1.00 for each additional book

Payment: Please make your check or money order payable to:

Small Potatoes Press
1106 Stokes Avenue, Collingswood, NJ 08108

Questions?   Call us at 856-869-5207 or e-mail us at info@smallpotatoespress.com

Ship to: Name _____

Address _____

City/State/Zip _____

Is this a gift? If so, please include YOUR name, address, and phone number.

Name _____

Address_____

City/State/Zip _____

Thank you!

About the Authors

Connie Correia Fisher is the owner of Small Potatoes Press which provides publishing and public relations support for restaurants and food-related businesses. She is the founding publisher/editor of *Cuizine* magazine and the author of *Philadelphia Flavor* and *PB&J USA*, America's only peanut butter and jelly cookbook.

Joanne Correia is Connie's mom and the former executive editor of *Cuizine*. She and Connie are the authors of *Local Flavor* and *Coastal Cuisine*.